*Letters from 74 rue Taitbout*

*Letters from*
*74 rue Taitbout*

or

# DON'T GO
# BUT IF YOU MUST
# SAY HELLO
# to EVERYBODY

by

## William Saroyan

THE WORLD PUBLISHING COMPANY
NEW YORK                    CLEVELAND

SIX OF THE LETTERS IN THIS BOOK—"ARMENAK OF BITLIS"; "CALOUSTE GULBENKIAN"; "THE MATCH GIRL"; "CARL SANDBURG"; "DR. HAROLD FRASER"; "DR. ANOUSHAVAN CHOMP"—APPEARED IN THE AUGUST 24, 1968, ISSUE OF THE SATURDAY EVENING POST

PUBLISHED BY THE WORLD PUBLISHING COMPANY
2231 WEST 110TH STREET, CLEVELAND, OHIO 44102

PUBLISHED SIMULTANEOUSLY IN CANADA BY
NELSON, FOSTER & SCOTT LTD.

FIRST PRINTING JANUARY, 1969

LIBRARY OF CONGRESS CATALOG CARD NUMBER: 69-16516

PRINTED IN THE UNITED STATES OF AMERICA

*To Yeghishe Charentz, Vahan Totoventz, and Gourken Mahari, poets, novelists, and playwrights of Armenia, and to their children and grandchildren.*

# *Contents*

# CONTENTS

*Letters from 74 rue Taitbout*

*To the Only One:* SEÑOR, MY HOUSE AT 74 RUE
Taitbout in the 9th arrondissement of Paris, just
beyond Trinité, is the fifth floor of this old building which I have come to believe in and to love, although it is falling to pieces.

There is an entry which is tiled, beyond
which is a narrow kitchen. The back part of the
house consists of a dining room, which I have never
used as such, beyond which is the bath, and finally
a large room in which I store junk-books and
other earthly treasures.

That leaves the front, which consits of two
rooms, each with a small fireplace.

My study is the room in which the fireplace

is dead. In the adjoining room there is a large pianola on top of which are stacks of books. There is also a draftman's stand with a large adjustable board which I use as an easel whenever I want to stand and paint.

I paint things to look at later, but these things do not look like other things unless the viewer insists on it.

"There," he says, "that's a horse, I think."

The opening of the double doors between the two front rooms makes them seem to be one room, which I like, for I like to go from my desk when my work is done to sit at a piano. I also like to stand and paint pictures on large pieces of inexpensive paper, using watercolors and needing scarcely two minutes to start and finish a picture. I also like having a second table to go to from time to time, to stand over, studying rocks, or to sit at and eat and drink, using an old newspaper as table covering, because there is always something interesting on a page, no matter which part of the paper it happens to be.

I have a small portable radio-phonograph in the second room, which I sometimes call the Music Room and sometimes the Library, saying to somebody or other, "Shall we repair to the Library?" I say the words as if I am in earnest, and so the other person imagines I am either poorly refined or some kind of nut.

❋  2  ❋

Beyond these two front rooms, which are almost one room and where I live and work, is perhaps the best part of the house—the whole width of the two rooms is given over to a kind of terrace, with a kind of lean-to or open shed at the far end in which logs are stored and where when the rain is heavy I can stand and see and hear and feel it. The terrace has a metal railing, quite neat in design and painted black. The width of the terrace is about five feet and the length about forty.

Others who have owned this place have put up bamboo fences for privacy, as the neighbors just across rue Taitbout can of course see whoever happens to be on the terrace. I have been told by the barber downstairs that one or two occupants have even put out plants and small trees in pots.

The fact is that when I first arrived here seven years ago I found a large roll of stick-fencing rotting in the corner of the lean-to. I used it for kindling one whole winter. And there were three old flowerpots, each with earth in it; so just a few days ago, finding that some garlic in the pantry was sprouting, I planted garlic in the pots and am waiting to see what happens.

Señor, please overlook my telling you these things at a time of such great trouble and dishonor in the world. I am sorry about the trouble and

❋ 3 ❋

the dishonor, but I just don't seem to be able to do anything about them, which, as you may remember, was what I set out to do when I began to be a writer almost fifty years ago.

*Armenak of Bitlis:* WELL, I VISITED YOUR GRAVE IN the cemetery by the railroad tracks in San Jose, California, earlier this year, and standing there on the numbered plot I remembered the first time I went there.

It was with your kid brother Mihran when I was seventeen or eighteen and he was thirty-seven or thirty-eight, forty years ago. Your brother wept standing there, and I with my big mouth, which I got from the other side of the family, from your wife, your widow, my mother, from the loud side of the family, I said, "What are you crying for, he's not here."

And I laughed, with the simple pleasure of

being in a place like that, on a grand day of summertime, because it was so good to be alive and because I didn't believe in death, couldn't believe in it, didn't believe you were dead, for instance, or that *anybody* had ever died.

Your brother was shocked by my remark and by my laughter, and not being able to speak clearly for the sobbing he was trying to control, he said, "Where is he, then?"

Well, this only made it worse, because Mihran always had a kind of earnestness and simplicity that put him to asking questions that were very funny to others.

"Oh, many places," I said. "No man ends in his grave, only his bones or his dust go there. A man stays forever where he had been. Where he was born, where he had his childhood and boyhood. He stays where he traveled, too, on the trains and ships, and he stays in the books he read. I have my father's books, he's all over the place in his books. I came here only to see where they put his bones. My father isn't dead. I'm here, so he's here, too." Well, of course, such theories are open to dispute, but that's beside the point.

For a long time I only remembered that little space in the grass, under the trees there, beside the road and (beyond the road) the railroad tracks. I didn't think or feel, "That's where my father is" or "That's where my father's bones lie" or anything like that. I only remembered that I had been there.

Now, as a small boy beginning to try to understand things, I believed that one day soon you would come walking up a street to me and know I was your son, aged three, four, five, six, seven, or eight. I went right on believing you would come walking until I was eleven or twelve, and then I forgot all about that idea. I didn't *disbelieve* it, I forgot about it, I let it go, and it stayed gone for a long time; and then all of a sudden it began to come back, and by that time I was a grown man.

I knew nothing but laughter, wild health, unquestioned confidence, ideas of all kinds day and night, and all kinds of interior and exterior movement, all kinds of going and coming. I started to travel as soon as I had the money for it, but the first big jaunt was financed by your kid brother Mihran, who loaned me $200 in 1928 just before I turned twenty, so I could go to New York by Greyhound bus. I paid him back of course, but he was always lending me new money even after I had earned twenty or thirty times as much as he ever did, and I was always paying him back, except once or twice when it took a number of years, and in the end I am afraid he may have loaned me more than I paid back.

I was all too well along in years, almost

as old as you were when you died in 1911, when I began to believe *again* that you would come walking up a street and find me.

Or rather than *believe* this would happen, I began to remember how I had long ago believed it would. "My father," I had thought, "he'll do that, because he's my father; he won't stay gone just because he's dead, he'll find a way to get back on his feet and come walking up a street and find me somewhere, because he's my father, and the way we are, we'll do a thing like that, we know it can't be done, it's against the law, but my father, he'll do that, and then what will the world think? What will people say? They'll say, 'He was dead for ten years, and then he came back, just like that, not a ghost, not somebody who looked like him, but himself, he came back, he came back to say his son's name,' that's what they'll say." And so it went, even when I was all over the place being myself so loudly and swiftly that total strangers in public places drew back in astonishment and sometimes even in fear, as if I myself were more than just one loud-mouthed laughing man.

And then one thing leading to another I forgot again for a long time. I remembered, but didn't pay very much attention to the remembering, because it was either not working or I hadn't grown with it to a new understanding of how it would happen, would *still* happen, after more than thirty years. All of a sudden in 1939 I became no longer tireless, no longer inexhaustible, and something happened to the laughter, the jokes, the noise, the going and coming, the travel, the eating, the drinking, the fun and the work and the fame and the money. I was thirty-one years old when I noticed a terrible sorrow in me wherever I went. Perhaps it was because the War was upon us again. I thought, "The streets are too cluttered for my father to come back now, he'd be lost in the hysteria, if we came face to face he wouldn't know me, he'd be terrified of everybody, and he'd be scared to death of me, too."

I found a little girl and married her and she gave birth to a son, and I looked at him and smelled him and listened to him and spoke to him, and something quite simple happened in my thinking, and this is what it was: "Here he is, and soon enough I'll see him walking up a street, and he'll stop and speak to me, just as I knew he would. This old man, already eight hours old, is my father."

But I let it go, I didn't think it would do, it wasn't quite the same thing, although there was in fact something to it that couldn't be totally dismissed.

After the War, when I saw my son again, he was two years old, but he didn't seem to know me, and I can't say I really knew him, either. In his earliest months his crying had troubled me, because it wasn't the way I had heard other small children cry.

When I got back from Europe, angry, confused, sick, desperate, as dead as I was alive, my son looked at me and burst into tears. The first thing I thought was, "It's my poor father, dead at the age of thirty-six, but back again, and all outraged. Is he mad at me for bringing him back? Have I been at fault in this? Has a crime been committed against him, by me?"

We broke up, but by that time there was a daughter to stand and walk beside the son, only they were with their mother, and I began to think, "Well, how are they, what's happening to them, how are they getting along, are they all right, will they be all right?"

By that time I was older than you ever were. The year was 1949. I was forty-one, and shot. I was *all* shot, all over the place, but that's all right, it happens all the time, it can happen to anybody, for all I know it has *got* to happen to everybody, but when it happens, and it's yourself, it's something else again, not something you can just talk about, it's what's going on, and it's killing, you've got to be very tough and very lucky to survive it.

For years I didn't go back to the little place in the San Jose graveyard, although I drove down the highway alongside the place and remembered the grave and now and then looked in that direction. I didn't think about any of it in that old way anymore, I just drove by, being followed by the broken pieces which were trying to catch up and get back together again.

And so it went for a long time. I sometimes woke with a start, as if from death, and tried to piece it all together, asking, "Now, wait a minute, where am I, where are my people, where's my father, where's my son?" And then little by little it would all come back and I would know what every man still alive knows, and I would get up and light a cigarette and pour whiskey into a glass and inhale smoke and swallow whiskey, and try to think.

I saw my son now and then, and his sister, and I spoke with him, and with her; but we were strangers, I really didn't know him, didn't know her, didn't know you, and didn't know myself.

And then one day in New York I was walking up Fifth Avenue from 44th Street. I had made a point of not writing to let my son know I would be in New York, because he so infrequently answered my letters, and when he did, his letters seemed strange. In one letter he even said my letters were a nuisance to him, so I didn't write anymore.

When I saw him coming down Fifth Avenue I knew he was my son, but it didn't matter, and I decided to walk by and let it go at that. It was all right, it happens all the time. Who's whose father? Is anybody anybody's father, isn't some crazy idea of the world itself every man's father? "He's fifteen years old now, he's as tall as I am now, he's coming toward me down Fifth Avenue, but I'll walk by, I'll see him, but he won't see me."

And then I thought, "It is in fact as if it were my father coming down a street as I always believed he would, only now I see him but he doesn't see me, so it'll be as if somebody in a crowd of people passed by, that's all, that's all it will be, and that's all right, too."

I kept looking at him as I walked, and when there was not more than four feet between us, among dozens of people, I saw him and he saw me, and I went on up Fifth Avenue, and he went on down. I didn't smile and he didn't smile. I didn't nod and he didn't nod. And I didn't care and I didn't care that he didn't care.

And then it happened, but not quite the way I had imagined for so long that it would.

I was walking straight ahead when somebody came running through the people to walk beside me, and when he reached me he almost shouted, "Pop."

I stopped, and he looked at me and said, "For God's sake, Pop, you passed me in the street. You saw me, but you didn't stop. I must have been dreaming or something, because I wasn't sure it was you, I thought it must be somebody else. Why didn't you stop, Pop? Why didn't you speak to me? Why didn't you say my name?"

I said, "Listen, my boy. Yes, I saw you, but you were going somewhere, and I didn't think I ought to stop you, I didn't think I ought to say your name. Now, I know you *are* going somewhere, so go ahead, because I am, too, and I've got to go."

I wasn't angry, and he knew I wasn't angry, and he understood.

"Can I call you at your hotel?"

"Any time."

He went on down Fifth Avenue and I went up.

I had been going to the same hotel for years, and he knew I always stopped there, and many hours later that day, it was around eleven at night, he called and we talked, and an hour later he came by and we went out and walked and talked.

Soon afterwards I went to Europe, and back and forth every year, and then one day when I

❋ 13 ❋

went back to San Francisco I found a letter from somebody at the State College in San Jose in which I was invited to go there soon and talk. And all of a sudden I remembered the little place in the graveyard in San Jose, and I answered the letter and said yes, I would go there for two or three days. When I got there I went straight out to the graveyard and into the office, and a lady got out the records and gave me the number of the place and told me how to get there, and I went there, I went to your grave, and I stood there looking down at the weedy grass.

I just wanted to stand there.

I remembered the first time I went there, with your kid brother Mihran, when he had stood there and had wept and I had laughed.

My father, standing there I was fifty-eight years old, my son was twenty-three, your kid brother had died the year before, aged seventy-seven, and your bones were still thirty-six years old. I'm not sure, I wouldn't care to swear to it, but I believe I said to myself, or thought, or felt, "Yes, my father is dead here."

I have an idea I was mistaken, but something like that is what I thought or said or felt or believed, but there was no sorrow in my heart. I guess it was because there hadn't been any when I was a little kid and believed you would come walking up a street someday and find me and say my name. Nothing exactly like that ever happened, but *something* happened. Nothing much can be made of it, most likely, but I thought I'd better mention it before I forget again.

*Dr. Freud, Dr. Jung, and Dr. Adler:* EVERY PERSON in the world is a character who deserves the kind of definitive biography that heirs authorize on behalf of famous men. Every person deserves the same thought and care that is given to the telling of the life of Winston Churchill, Franklin Delano Roosevelt, Benito Mussolini, Adolf Hitler, Joseph Stalin, or any other famous man. But of course everybody doesn't get what he deserves in the way of a written life. He himself can't write his life, he can't imagine it, he can't think it, and nobody else will do these things for him.

Such a loss is a pity, although it is not nearly the pity other losses are: the loss of one's own life in a war, for instance; or the loss of mind in whole generations of people from continuous insecurity, doubt, harassment, fear, anxiety, and naggings of all kinds, by all kinds of things that everybody expects everybody to become adjusted to—governments, taxes, wars, and the draft, which is imposed upon the young without consultation with them, or their approval.

Now, of course all his life everybody adjusts, from the minute he's out in the open to the minute he rolls back into the closed.

He adjusts.

It gets to be his nature to adjust. He even begins to believe he likes to adjust. It breaks the monotony. It gives him a kind of reason for being. He adjusts himself into a total incapacity to find out who he is and what he might do about it. He is not himself, he is his adjustments, he is a product manufactured by his government.

All of which makes him the character I mentioned a moment ago. His body changes as he adjusts, his posture changes, the way he stands and walks changes, his nerves change, his brain changes, his very cells change. And for want of something better to do to help him get through another difficult moment of another hopeless day he lights a cigarette, inhales deeply, and feels again he might just make it safely to the other side.

Dr. Freud, Dr. Jung, Dr. Adler, what is this poor man to do—for himself, for the human race, for nature, for art, for truth, for God? Nothing? Adjust until he finally adjusts to stupid death? Does *he* count, at all, or is it only yourselves, ourselves, the superior ones, the lucky ones, the talented ones, who count?

I ask the question on behalf of the poor man himself, with his desperate posture, his shot nervous system, his failing blood, his bad breath.

Everybody has bad breath. In America the business of manufacturing, advertising, and selling mouthwashes that are supposed to banish bad breath is very big. Billions of dollars every year are involved. Millions of people keep washing out their mouths with dozens of different kinds of liquids that are worth six cents a bottle, including advertising in newspapers and magazines, on radio and television, but sell for ninety-six cents, reduced from one dollar and fifty cents. And still their bad breath keeps coming to them. They also sweat, and they are told that it is a very bad thing to sweat, so they spray themselves to stop the sweat, to shut the pores, or to neutralize the smell, or to replace it with the smell of violets. Well, nobody has ever smelled like a violet unless he has lived on a diet of violets for a week or two. Statesmen, the members of the governments of the world, have bad breath. And they sweat, and they smell, and they must be reminded by their wives, daughters, secretaries, or friends, "For God's sake, Mr. President, you have bad breath." Of course Mr. President has bad breath, he's just as human and harassed as everybody else, why wouldn't he have bad breath? He gets his bad breath from his work, from the tensions of the decisions he has got to make, from what he eats and drinks and smokes.

But some people *don't* have bad breath, and there was a time when the mouths of the girls of the world tasted like cool milk and sometimes like little flowers. And it wasn't from mouthwashes or sweat-replacements, it was from themselves, from their bodies, from their youth, from their health, and even from their ignorance, or their innocence. But these girls after five or six years began to have bad breath, too, and had to cover their body smells with all kinds of perfume. Something happened to them. Love didn't work out as they had every reason to believe that it would.

When the girls have sweet breath, the young men who love them believe that that is how love is going to be forever. But soon it's not so, the girls stink, and the boys stink. Well, did the world do it, did nature do it, or did it happen because their minds wandered? (Eskimos and other Asiatics who live hard lives stink all the time and never give it a thought. They have other things to think about, and their kids are born as sound and right as kids ever are.)

Now, kids all over the world, excepting possibly the kids of the Eskimos and other Asiatic tribes, are beginning to *let* themselves stink, on purpose, and this is something everybody is thinking about, because the stinking part of it isn't *all* of it, it's only a little of what they are really doing. They seem to be trying not to be sucked into the losing game which they sense has got to cost them everything: truth, freedom, love, and life itself. A lot of them are feebleminded, but they are only the ones who would have become bankers, lawyers, and politicians. There are always more of the feebleminded than of the strong-minded, so it doesn't matter at all that a lot of the kids who won't work and won't give up pot or LSD happen to be feebleminded. Why shouldn't they be, their fathers and mothers were, weren't they? What did they expect, another Dr. Freud, another Dr. Jung, another Dr. Adler?

Gentlemen, *you* did not compel this revolt of the young. These sons and daughters of men and women of all kinds, including the inferior and feebleminded, have somehow gotten around to it by themselves. They just don't want to adjust. They ask, "Adjust to *what?*"

How did it happen? Out of a world full of characters, each of them worthy of a definitive life but each of them totally ignored, how did these new characters come to pass? How did it happen that all of a sudden there was a whole new world happening among the young?

I'll tell you how it happened, because I know. It was an act of nature. It happened by itself, because it had to happen. The breed is protecting itself from itself. It doesn't want to become extinct.

Bad breath isn't anywhere near as bad as no breath at all.

*Hovagim Saroyan:* I REMEMBER STAYING OVERNIGHT at your vineyard on the north side of Fresno, to which my brother Henry and I traveled with you in a carriage drawn by an old horse. I know the distance from our house at 2226 San Benito Avenue to your vineyard was only four miles, as I have made the journey recently several times, but it seemed to us a far greater distance.

Henry and I sat in the back like passengers, and you sat on the higher seat up front, none of us speaking, perhaps because your language was Armenian and ours was English, although we *could* speak Armenian, too. But mainly we were not speaking because we were glad to be together, traveling. It was late in the afternoon of a hot day, and you came to our house and said to our mother, "Takoohi, let me take the boys to the ranch, I will take them jackrabbit shooting, we will have supper, we will listen to old country records, and I will bring them back tomorrow in time for church. I don't want to ride home alone." And my mother said, "Hovagim, if you want them to go with you, take them." And so we went.

It was 1917, exactly fifty years ago, perhaps this very same month, July, and you were alone out there on the vineyard. Your wife and two sons were in Bitlis or near there or far from there, if they weren't dead, if they hadn't been killed, or hadn't died of hunger and thirst on the long march from Bitlis to the desert which so many others made and in which so many died. But even if they were alive, you hadn't heard from them or from anybody who had seen them. Perhaps the boys were alive, but didn't know who they were, having been too little to remember, having been taken to an orphanage and given new names.

I used to know you were alone, even before I heard about what had happened, heard my mother telling somebody.

You came to America, to work, to send money to your wife, so she and your sons could come too, but it didn't work out that way. You sent money and letters, and your wife replied, and then she didn't reply, and a whole year went by, and then another whole year went by, and you didn't know what had happened. You had an idea, but you didn't know for sure. You were alone everywhere I ever saw you, even in the Arax Coffee House full of card players. I knew you were alone the first time I saw you sitting in our parlor sipping a cup of coffee, so when you said, "I don't want to go home alone," I knew what you were talking about, the way a small boy will know such a thing and never be able to talk about it.

Riding in the back of your carriage, on our way to your vineyard and your little house there, I kept wondering what it was that had *most* made you alone, and I thought it must be from not having your father with you, because that's how we think, I guess, out of what is true for each of us, out of whatever each of us knows that makes us alone. Your father and my mother's father were brothers, and I knew my mother's father had died in Bitlis and, dying, had said to my mother's mother, "Get the family out of here, leave this place, go anywhere else, but do not stay here any longer, go to America if you can manage."

And of course she *did* manage, although it wasn't easy: the people who control the papers and the rubber stamps had to be bribed with gold one by one, and then transportation had to be paid for, first by donkey train over high mountains along narrow roads from Bitlis to Erzeroum, where my brother Henry was born in 1905, and from Erzeroum to Trabizon, where a ship carried them to Constantinople, and then to Marseilles, where they all had to work to raise money for the train ride across France to Le Havre, where again they had to work until there was enough money to put everybody on the ship that sailed to New York—a long crossing, far below in the ship, in steerage, where hundreds of families prepared their own meals and made sleeping places on the floor, followed at last by the fear and the terror of Ellis Island. Everybody was "bono" except Lucy, my mother's mother herself, and somebody with a rubber stamp said she would have to go back to Bitlis. The whole family went mad. The situation was unbelievable for hours, in which the heart died in everybody, and the old woman, then scarcely forty years of age, said, "Do not despair. God will put forth his hand." And the next day her eyes were examined again, and almost as if it meant nothing, nothing at all, somebody else with a rubber stamp stamped her papers and said, "Bono." And thus the family was not deprived of its force, authority, intelligence, wisdom, and faith.

What had made you so alone? I kept wondering what had made us all so alone, even when many of us were together, and what it was,

I felt, was at least partly the people with the power, with the papers, with the rubber stamps, the enforcers of the rules and regulations, a whole world full of such people. They scare a man. They are killers.

After we finally arrived at your vineyard you took us to your cow and milked her and invited us to drink fresh milk. It was warm and seemed all right, but an hour later, while we were out jackrabbit hunting, we both threw up. We saw a couple of the big loping jackrabbits but they were too far away to shoot, and then we came back to your little shack house, and you served us a good dinner of stuffed tomatoes, bell peppers, and cucumbers, with flat bread and yogurt. And then we sat down in your parlor while you played Armenian records on the wind-up phonograph. The music was proud, beautiful, and lonely. And then we both began to fall asleep and you got us to our beds.

Hovagim, sleeping in your house was something I couldn't understand when I woke up in the morning. There was a smell of sorrow and loneliness in my nostrils, and I couldn't remember where I was, but I knew I wasn't in my own bed in my own home. And then I remembered. I was at Hovagim's house. I got dressed and went out and ate figs straight from the big tree, and then my brother Henry came out, and he ate some figs, too. And he said, "It feels funny sleeping in somebody else's house, doesn't it?" And I said, "Did you feel it, too?"

Pretty soon we saw you coming from your ditch where you had been guiding water to your vines, and you said in English, "All right, boys, now we eat." And you fixed us tea and fried dough, or new bread, into which we stuffed white cheese, and we ate boiled eggs and slices of dried beef, and lots of parsley and mint and fresh tomatoes and cucumbers sliced lengthwise.

And then you harnessed the old horse to the carriage and we set out for home. That's all, Hovagim. But it was one of the great experiences of my life, don't ask me why. It just was. I guess it was your kindness and aloneness. It certainly wasn't the milk fresh from the cow—that stuff's poison.

I saw you around town for a couple more years, and then all it was was a matter of remembering.

I hope both of the boys got out of it alive, even if they lost their names, because under any name I think they would be O.K.

*Calouste Gulbenkian:* WHEN I ARRIVED AT THE Avis Hotel in Lisbon, in May of 1949 I was surprised to learn that you occupied all of the mezzanine floor.

"Gulbenkian?" I said to the manager of the hotel. "Do you mean the man who is rich?"

"The richest man in the world," the manager of the hotel said. "He is Armenian, as I believe you are."

I was forty-one years old at the time, and in a bad way, having just left my wife, small son, and smaller daughter, for reasons that were grave enough to make my leaving imperative.

I was in a state of spiritual shock. I missed

something. I could say it was my wife, my son, and my daughter, but I'm afraid it was something else—I missed the truth. I was suddenly without home, continuity, and meaning. I was without myself, my own ghost. I was not only lost, I was cut down. I was in fact dead. But I *seemed* to be alive. If anything, more alive than ever, from not knowing what to do next, or where to go, in order to start being alive in the truth again.

You were almost twice my age, and in vigorous good health. You mentioned during lunch that your father had lived to be ninety-eight and that you believed you would live at least that long, too. The money that came to you daily from oil leases which you had negotiated on behalf of countries having the oil and countries wanting to buy it did not stop four years later when you did, however. Money flows in secret rivers in many different places, from somewhere to somebody, and the river that had flowed to you for so long continued to flow after your death at eighty-four to the Foundation you established in Lisbon.

At that time Russia was putting pressure on Iran and Irak, and there appeared to be a chance that these countries would be taken into the Soviet Socialistic body of nations, whereupon the flow of the rivers would be diverted from you to the Soviet government or to the people of Iran and Irak.

I tend to ask anybody I am with simple questions, not in rudeness but in the interest of truth, and so I asked if such a condition would come to you as a blow, or a sorrow, and you replied, "Oh no, if it happens, I shall not mind at all. It will be all right, not so much because in any event I am not a poor man, but rather because change of one sort or another is always happening and unavoidable, and there is no reason for me to regret any change that affects my interests. It may even be a good thing—for me, even. I might find time to concern myself more with art—I love great paintings, for instance. And the money involved might be put to better use than I might ever manage, although I have great numbers of skilled people working on the problem of how best to put to work the money that has come to me."

The richest man in the world, or at any rate one of the richest men in the world, speaking to me in this manner, in the Armenian language as well as now and then in English, pleased me, for I have always believed that money ought not to go to a few lucky people in the world as long as there is poverty of any kind among the majority of the people. In short, you were speaking both truthfully and honorably about your good luck in having had the skill of negotiation which had started the making of your great fortune.

Because of my own particular astonishment and anxiety at that time I listened carefully to everything you said. You had no idea how things were with me, although you may have suspected that something was wrong. I know I do when I am in the company of somebody in some kind of trouble. On the one hand, it really didn't matter that you happened to be an Armenian, and on the other, it pleased me deeply that you were, for I needed to see somebody in the family, so to put it. I needed to talk to somebody who might very well be almost a relative, and while I didn't think of you as a father, or somebody who was something like a father, I did feel that there was a real connection between us. We had almost nothing in common, and yet we were instantly related: it happened when you surprised and pleased me by speaking a dialect of Armenian that was no trouble at all for me to understand, and I was delighted to notice that you instantly understood my replies in the dialect of Bitlis.

In a sense, we were both homeless, we had no geographical country of our own as we had once had and as we had ever since *wanted* to have, excepting the very small portion of what was once our country, which had become a part of Soviet Russia in 1921.

By nature, neither of us could make a life there, if in fact we would *want* to, even had we had our own independent nation. You had made your way in Istanbul, in Tehran, in Mosul, in Baghdad, in London, in Paris, in Lisbon, and in many of the other cities of the world. And in a sense I was making my way in much the same manner, starting in California, moving on to New York, and from there to Europe, and to Soviet Armenia in 1935.

We simply did not belong to a geographical and political country that was our own. We lived and worked here and there, but it was known that you were Armenian and that I was Armenian, and at lunch we acknowledged to each other instantly that we were. We spoke our language, and enjoyed doing so.

I was pleased when you said, "The waiters who are paid to pass along things I say in English, French, Portuguese, and other languages shall be very puzzled today. Very few people in the world make a point of learning the Armenian language. In a moment you will observe the headwaiter as he comes to this table to move a fork or pour wine, but actually to listen to our speech, and to wonder what language it is. I speak Turkish and Arabic as well, of course, and he has heard me do so, but he has never heard me speak Armenian. I shall enjoy his bewilderment."

And sure enough, the headwaiter did in fact come to our table and very slowly pour wine, as you said in Armenian, "Let us please keep talking, I want him to hear the Armenian language being spoken."

And simply to comply with your request I said, "But he knows you are Armenian, and he will presume that we are speaking that language, won't he?" And you said, "Well, it is one thing to know we are speaking the Armenian language, but another to know what we are saying. He is paid to pass along information about anything I happen to say that he hears and understands, but what information can he sell this time?"

I said, "He can certainly say an Armenian from America had lunch with you today, but no business of any kind was discussed or transacted—they just ate and drank and spoke Armenian."

And then the waiter was obliged to go back to his watchful place, and you said, "I am glad you have come to Lisbon, but how did you happen to come to this hotel? People reserve rooms a year in advance, and there are very few rooms to be had."

"At the airport I asked the taxi driver to take me to the best hotel in Lisbon," I said. "And the taxi driver said in Portuguese, which I neither speak nor understand but nevertheless understood when he spoke it: 'Well, the best is the Avis, but it is very expensive.' And so I came here. Ribeira, the manager, at first told me there was no room, but after a glance at my passport, he asked me to wait five or ten minutes. And then he said, 'Room 404,' and I must say I like the room very much, especially the tile floor and walls and halls, tile everywhere."

We had lunch the following day, too, and

❄ 33 ❄

dinner several times, and you began to suspect that
something was the matter, for I was hungover every
day, and went by taxi every afternoon and again
every evening to the casino at Estoril and gambled
—winning and losing, and losing, and winning, and
drinking all the time, and of course there were
pretty women there to be taken somewhere, so that
between the gambling, drinking, and women I
decided it didn't matter any more; it was all right,
I really didn't care that I was dead, homeless, lost,
and forty-one years old. I don't know how you
found out, but one day at lunch you said, "In all
the years I have been in Lisbon, I have never set
foot in the casino at Estoril. If it happens that
you need money, please let me know." I must
say I was dumbfounded, both that you knew I
was spending so much time at the casino and that
you nevertheless wanted to help me—even with
money. But I am the Saroyan I am. I pay my own
way. I make mistakes and pay for them. I am not
permitted to accept money from others for any
purpose or reason. I said, "Thank you very much,
I am all right. I have everything." But that very
night my luck (if there is in fact such a thing
when a man is drowning) was incredible, both
when it was good and when it was bad, so that in
the end I didn't even have money enough to
leave the casino with one of the women there.
And almost nothing in Room 404, only a few

dollars, and one gold coin worth about fifty dollars, and there was still the hotel bill to pay. The next day at the casino I exchanged the gold coin for enough chips to at least begin to play carefully, but sooner or later I cannot do anything carefully, and I began to bet everything I had in one play, and to win, too. And so it went for the next two or three hours. And then I had enough money both for the hotel and to take a train to Biarritz. I didn't want to fly, I wanted to sit in a train and try to think.

I won't say anything about gambling, except that it has been a part of my life from the beginning. In money I have been a winner many times, but in money I am a heavy loser over the years. In other things, happening at the same time as the gambling, I have been a winner, including writing. During our meetings at lunch and dinner we talked about many things, a hundred times more than the few things I have here remembered, and during our last lunch we touched upon the future, knowing I was taking a train the following morning and we might not meet again for a long time, if ever. Again you said, "If you need anything, anything at all, please tell me." And again I thanked you and said I was just fine.

At Biarritz I gambled again, but the rampage was over and if I won, it was money of the kind that one counts and puts against things one can pay for as one goes along, and if I lost, it was only a small part of what I had, so I knew the worst was over.

I didn't like Biarritz, but I didn't dislike it, either. It was not at all like Lisbon and Estoril, both of which I loved. I may say I instantly liked the Portuguese people, who are mainly poor, but stand and walk with a kind of elegance and pride that I was deeply moved by, children, men, women, and even very old men and women. And they had faces upon which were engraved the lines of deep sorrow, gentility, honor, and courtesy. For instance, when the taxi arrived at the Avis, not knowing the value of the Portuguese money, I made a guess and put quite a variety of coins into the hand of the taxi driver. He protested, or at any rate (having lately come from Rome) I imagined that he had protested and I began to bring out more money, but his protest had been that I had put *too much* money into his hand. He picked out a number of the more valuable coins and handed them back to me. I was deeply moved, for in Rome, no matter how much I gave a taxi driver, he immediately cried that he could not live unless people were more generous, he had a wife and many children, and so on and so forth. And of course I found myself frequently at Machado's for food and drink, and to listen to the men and women who sang fado, which so suited my own condition at the time.

In Biarritz it was another story entirely: the casino was a boring place, the players were cautious and pompous, and there didn't seem to be any women I cared to look at twice.

I went on to Paris and stopped at the Scribe. One of the reasons I did so was that Scribe to me means "to write," and I felt my best chance of getting myself back together again was to write, and I went there because during my first visit to Paris, in 1935, I had gone into the hotel just to have a look at it, and finally in 1945, when I had been in the American Army, the Scribe had been a popular hangout for foreign correspondents, photographers, and writers. Almost every night at the Scribe there had been a poker game in which I took a seat, finally losing three thousand dollars to my friend Robert Capa.

I had an outside room, and it seemed to me to be just right for going to work—a top-floor room with a sloping ceiling, like an attic.

I hoped to do a novel, for I needed money— not immediately, but in the future: a divorce coming up, two small kids to support, and so on and so forth. I didn't wait, I brought out the portable typewriter, I put paper beside it, a sheet of paper upon the rubber roller, and I began to write, simultaneously glad that I was at least *trying* to get back together and *disbelieving* in the possibility of it, even. (What could I write?) The going was rough, but I kept at it, and then after five or six days I stopped, I had had enough.

What I had written was not a novel, but it was a long short story, and it was about you, and it was about me, and the name of it was "The Assyrian."

My mother's kid brother had a son who was living in Paris at that time with his bride, and he had read in the *Herald* that I had come to town and was stopping at the Scribe, so one afternoon he came up to the room to talk. I had known him from the time of his birth, when I had been ten or eleven years old. I was glad to see him again, to hear about his adventures during four years in the Navy.

And then he said, "How come you're traveling alone?"

I told him I had left my wife and kids, and then he said, "Tell me all about it, will you?"

But I couldn't, and then he said, "What do you think of *my* marriage?" I didn't understand, and told him so.

He then said, "I mean, I'm here in Paris with my wife, I'm trying to write, and she's trying to write, too."

I told him that that sounded all right to me.

We went down to the street and walked to where he was living in an attic somewhere on the Left Bank, and I sat and chatted with his wife.

And then the three of us went to dinner

nearby, and after dinner he brought a manuscript out of his back pocket, a rather thick manuscript, folded as if for slipping into an envelope and mailing, and he said, "Will you read this, please, right now, right here, and tell me honestly if I can write, if I ought to go on, or if I ought to forget it?"

Well, it was a kind of short novel, but it wasn't easy to read because he hadn't cleaned the type on his machine, and all of the vowels looked alike. All the same, I read the story very carefully, and although it was badly written, it *was* a story— of confusion, sorrow, ignorance, doubt, and the state of being lost. As I read I tried to think how I would speak to him about what he had written, and he smoked one cigarette after another, compelling me to say, "I read very slowly, please be patient, I don't want to miss any of it," and then at last I came to the last word, and he very nearly leaped at me, saying, "Tell me, tell me the truth, don't tell me any lies."

I don't think I told him any lies when I said, "Well, the writing *does* lack skill, it has no real style, but that's all right, don't worry about that, skill and style will come if you write enough, the important thing is that the story is a very good one, a very important one, but don't write it again, study it, revise it carefully, perhaps salvage it, but at the same time move on to a new work."

"Am I a writer?" he said, and of course the

proper answer to that question would be, "If you can ask such a question, you are not a writer," but I didn't say that. I said, "I think you are. I would like to ask you to find it in yourself to believe you are, because if you don't believe that, your writing will show it."

We walked about a mile to a vaudeville theater and went in, and after the show we sat at a sidewalk table and drank whiskey and smoked cigarettes and talked.

Now, the point about my cousin is this: his story had things in it that were also in the story I had just finished writing, "The Assyrian," about yourself and myself, and at the same time about other people, and other things, so that I was impelled to think, "My cousin's in trouble, too, he's in a lot of trouble. What's eating *him*?"

After having lived in Paris with his wife for two years, they returned to the United States, because she was pregnant and she wanted the child to be born in California. One day when I ran into him in Fresno, he said, "I just read your new book, *The Assyrian and Other Stories,* and the best thing in it is the title story, but why did you call Gulbenkian an Assyrian? Why didn't you call the story 'The Armenian'?"

I said, "It comes to the same thing. The Assyrians have always been close to us, and lately almost the same thing."

"I don't understand," he said. "Everything in the story is so true, and then it turns out the writer has made the two main characters Assyrian, and they're not Assyrian, they're Armenian."

But he was saying something else, only I wasn't sure I knew what it was. But I knew he was in trouble, *still* in trouble, his son was two years old, and his wife had just given birth to a daughter, and these things didn't seem to have done anything for him that all of us, Armenians, Assyrians, and everybody else, have always believed would do *everything* for us.

"It's one of your best stories," he said. "Maybe it's the best one you've ever written or ever will write, why call them Assyrians?"

"Well, all right," I said at last. "I guess I goofed. I won't do it again."

He roared with laughter, shouting, "No, no, that's not what I mean, God damn it, I'm not giving you a lecture, I just wish you had called them what they are, that's all." But he didn't say anything about his own writing, and I had heard he had tried operating a vineyard but hadn't liked it and had gotten out of it, and then had taken a kind of unbelievable job for a while in a big department store, selling shoes. But he had given that up, too.

Well, what's he got to do with us? This. He was, he is, he always will be, one of us. Shall I say homeless? No, the hell with that. Lost? No, he was no more lost than anybody else in the world. I really don't know what I should say, except that he was in so much trouble that for ten years he kept going to places for all kinds of treatments— shock and pills and whatever else the confused doctors and psychiatrists happened to believe in at the time—and finally he started trying another way out, and then at last he made it, the hard way: divorced by that time, his kids out of sight for years by that time, the car that he was forever washing and waxing and rubbing until it looked like a little blue jewel fell slowly over a small cliff near Piedra upon an abandoned railroad track in gasoline flames, himself a jumping and running torch. And then lying upon thick grass, asking for water, saying with annoyance to the girl who had seen his car go over the cliff, "What are these people here for?" And then to the highway patrol cop who pushed his way through the people, "Are you going to kill me?" And hours later at the Veterans Hospital, when he was no longer anything anybody ought to look at, he kept saying, "I'm not going to die, am I?" And early in the morning he did, he died, forty-four years old, God have mercy on his soul.

I probably goofed saying we were Assyrians, but not really, because in a sense everybody in the world is an Assyrian, a remnant of a once-mighty race, now all but extinct.

*Guy de Maupassant:* I REMEMBER WANDERING
around one afternoon at Fresno Technical High
School, where I was learning typing, eleven or
twelve years old, in 1919 or 1920, desperate as only
a man of that many years can be, angry at something or somebody, alone in spirit, bored, and
hoping that I might find in the library something
to speak to me.

I found a story called "The Bell." I sat
down and began to read it, not knowing what it
was or what effect it was going to have on me.

Guy de Maupassant, your story told me to
write, and that's all I needed to know.

Six or seven years ago your specialist, Artine

Artinian, an editor and translator, wrote to writers all over the world inviting them to say what your writing meant to them. Many were faithful, or at any rate almost so, but many more were almost embarrassed that they had ever been deeply moved by your writing or had ever cherished it.

Well, the hell with them. I remain faithful.

Your writing is your writing. Nobody else has ever written in that *living* manner, and every writer who has ever read your writing has been improved by it.

I thank you again, as I do every year.

*The Match Girl:* DEAR LITTLE SILLY LITTLE ridiculous little girl of only thirty years ago, you were eighteen then, from York, Pennsylvania, in Hollywood to be a star, with a secret unrevealed in your belly. How we happened to meet I can't remember, but all of a sudden there you were living in my apartment at the Villa Carlotta, a kind of swanky place for new arrivals in the writing departments of the moviemaking business. There you were in the last days of the best month of the year, October, 1936, sharing my life, the life of a new American writer, twenty-eight years old, famous from coast to coast, as the saying is, two books published in New York, London, Paris, Berlin, Rome, and a lot of other places, but for all that a loud and desperate man, gone to Hollywood in a decrepit Packard to earn some quick money, with which to pay some foolish debts.

Every now and then over the years I have wondered about you, but even more about the child which revealed itself soon after you settled down with me, not mine, a boy's in Pennsylvania before you decided to go West, going in fact because you knew something had caught and was started and you didn't want to marry him, couldn't tell your father and mother, didn't know what to do, but didn't want an abortion. And then in mid-December we talked about the whole thing, and you agreed that you ought to go home, tell your parents, and have the baby—a girl, you wrote and said.

Where is she now, that is what I have wondered about every now and then. Her mother was eighteen or nineteen when the little girl was born, so she's thirty now, how many kids does *she* have, how is it going with *her*?

And then one day in Ohio, just after I had gotten married, walking to the cafeteria at Wright Field, there you were in some kind of work clothes women wore in those days, and I said, "What are you doing *here*?" And you said, "Making movies." You were still making movies of some kind, twenty-five years old now. "To win the war." Which in fact you *did* win. I certainly didn't, and then once again I was in Hollywood, in 1947, not to work, only to loaf around, to go to Santa Anita for the races, and one evening walking up Hollywood Boulevard on my way to Stanley Rose's bookstore, there you were again, but not alone this time, with a boy who was not a movie man of any kind, not a producer, director, cameraman, casting director, grip, messenger, or anything else, just a boy from out of town trying his luck in Hollywood, too, and you broke away from him to say, "I'm back, I'm back, I couldn't stay away, this is the only place for me," twenty-nine years old, with a daughter ten years old. "She's with my mother, they love each other, she's a little beauty, and she's made my mother very happy. Can you get me a part in a movie?"

And of course I couldn't. Who could? It wasn't that you couldn't act, it was just that so many others were ahead of you and had the kind of friends who could manage it, at least halfway.

I couldn't. And I couldn't even begin to pretend that I could, for whatever might be in it for you, or even for me, although for a flash I was tempted and wanted to have you again, but wouldn't even tell you quickly to phone me at the Plaza.

And then one last time I saw you in a place where I never believed I'd see you, in New York, walking near Tiffany's with an old man I knew wasn't your father, and I saw you go into Tiffany's with him, and that was it, I didn't see you again.

You were a sweet little girl, little girl with a little girl in your belly, and I really loved you and loved her, and still do. I love both of you, although there is really little reason to do so, and I think I know why I love you, why I love both of you. You are of that family of girls who live a whole large uncaring life of earnestness, misunderstanding, desire, expectancy, failure, laughter, and indifference. You are not clever, your sisters who are clever and marry clever and divorce clever and use their children clever will tell you how stupid you really are, but in the end you have lived a life and they have lived a lie. That's why I love you and still wonder about you, and your daughter, and your daughter's daughter, may your tribe increase.

*Prof-Kalfayan:* LITTLE OLD IMMORTAL UNKNOWN roly-poly, let me tell you a story about yourself.

Who *is* that coming up Van Ness Avenue looking like some kind of bogus prince from some preposterous place of fantasy somewhere in the world, waxed black moustache, waxed black goatee, cane, spats, black Bohemian hat, black suit, black cape, who can that possibly *be* in Fresno, in 1918, coming straight to the corner where I'm selling *The Evening Herald?* Did anybody ever before see anybody like that, let alone an Armenian? Who is he, what is he, what's he doing in this faraway little town of grapes, raisins, peaches, apricots, figs, olives, almonds, walnuts, vineyards, orchards, churches, coffeehouses, memories, anger, sorrows, and rage, who is this bouncing cane-swinging roly-poly ball of black fire, bearing down on me with dark eyes all aflame?

You, of course, that's who. A boulevardier, fresh from Paris, a star pupil of the great Vincent d'Indy, come to Fresno to compose and conduct liturgical music for our true church, and patriotic songs for fathers and mothers and their boys and girls. The thunder-voiced lunatic with the manu-factured hyphenated highfalutin name: Prof-Kal-fayan.

Well, of course, it just wouldn't do, such a character had no place in our fighting society, anybody could see he was a phony, pompous and pretentious, and so what could I do except stare and show my contempt?

And then you paused ever so slightly to look at me, but not to stare back, not to answer my con-tempt with annoyance, you only hesitated long enough to let me know you had noticed me, and in a loud voice you said in Armenian, "Shout, my boy, you are an Armenian." And off you went across the street to the post office, old Huff the Popcorn Man watching you with his one good eye, and everybody else in the street stopping to watch, too.

Prof, you were something, you were really something out of some kind of misplaced folklore, a kind of phony from the beginning to the end, but all the same something grand, too, something large and dark and mad and lonely and desperately sad.

In spite of your strange greeting, and in fact partly on account of it, I disliked you. You were an Armenian, but the hell with that. You weren't the kind of Armenian I could care about, and there were a lot of Armenians of that kind, more than of any other kind, more than of the kind I cared for, took pride in, cherished, and loved. And a lot of these unacceptable Armenians were in my own family. I disliked you at sight, little old roly-poly. What the hell was the cape for? Who did you think you were? Where did you think you were?

And then little by little word got around about who you were and where you were from, and a lot of the kids of Armenian Town who went to the red-brick church said you were teaching them how to sing, how to really sing. They said you scared them with your loud voice and your black face and eyes, but they did confess that they were learning to sing. They also said you could sit at the piano and play music, strange music, new music, but somehow still Armenian. And you could sit at the church organ and make it thunder like a bull or sob like a brokenhearted young girl.

Even so, I went right on disliking you, because you were a phony, I thought. Well, of course you were, you were the biggest phony in the whole town, but you were also precisely who you were, a man of music, a composer, with a very difficult job to do at the church, both for the wages you were paid and for the life of the church itself, the life of the people, the life of the nation, shattered, dispersed, wounded, broken, one part out of touch with the other, and everybody trying desperately to make a living and to go on being Armenian at the same time.

Matters didn't improve when my mother decided I had better go to Armenian school and learn to read and write, and you were there with Holy Father Casparian, teaching the alphabet and simple phrases, and loud singing. I began to suspect you had a hard job to do, but it didn't improve matters for me, I still didn't like you.

Some of your patriotic songs reached our house on San Benito Avenue both as sheet music and on records, and I listened to the records, and every song I heard was strange and proud, but I needed to hear each of them six or seven times before I began to feel you were more than I had at first believed. And in less than two years, as news from Armenia reached me, and we knew we had lost, we had again lost, your cape was gone, your Bohemian hat was gone, the Paris shoes and spats were gone, you no longer carried a stick, and whenever you came up Van Ness Avenue to my corner you looked like another forlorn Armenian, and I began to think twice about who you were and what you were doing, and about the way I felt about you. I began to believe I was mistaken about you.

On special church days I went to the red-brick church instead of to the First Armenian Presbyterian Church, and I saw you in robes leading the choir of boys and girls, and playing the organ, and I knew almost all of the music was your own, which you had especially composed for the church.

Your little house, provided by the church, was on the alley our house was on, yours a block north of ours, and so I passed it many times on my way to town, and almost always heard you at the piano, working, and sometimes singing. And now and then I saw you standing like a farmer on the front porch, apparently thinking, although God knows what.

When I was seventeen, old man, and getting ready to make my getaway from that town, from our old neighborhood in Armenian Town, you were surely thirty-five or maybe forty, and you were not getting ready to make your getaway; you were there to stay, and it seemed to me that that may have been the reason why, whenever I saw you standing on the front porch, you seemed so lost and confused and alone. Having studied in Paris, having known Vincent d'Indy and surely many many others—composers, poets, painters, students, and the pretty girls these people always know—it couldn't have been easy for you to live where you now lived. I heard the stories of your regular visits to the little upstairs hotels on Broadway, where the girls were. I had been to those hotels delivering telegrams and I knew they were dismal, depressing places, nothing like the same sort of thing in Paris.

I made my getaway, and I stayed away, going back only once in a long while, to see members of the family, but always I couldn't wait to go away again. On one visit a young cousin and I were driving around to the nearby towns, Fowler, Selma, Kingsburg, Del Rey, Sanger, Yettem, when all of a sudden my cousin began to sing at the top of his voice your patriotic song about the dark horseman coming out of the hills, and I said, "How is the little old roly-poly guy? Let's go see him."

It was a hot summer day, and we found you in bare feet, fatter than ever, and sweating a little. The inside of your house, which I saw that day for the first time, was a bedlam of sheet music, books, papers, Armenian magazines, pictures of soldiers, priests, old friends, dead friends, and years of dust over everything. For some reason you spoke in French, imagining I must know that language, being a writer, and you said, "Saroyan, do not abandon me." You said it many times, and I really didn't know what you were talking about, except that you were quite plainly drowning and awfully scared. You were trapped and tied and losing your breath, and you kept saying, "Saroyan, pas abandonnee, moi." I didn't know French then, and I don't know it now, even though I am now in Paris and have spent most of the past eight years here. I'm no good at languages. I feel lucky that I am able to use English a little. I was loaded with loot in those days, and anything I didn't understand about anybody I believed must be the consequence of a need of money, so I put some currency on your table where I believed you would find it, and my cousin and I said good-bye.

Two years later I visited you in your house again, and the situation was the same, only worse. You were dying, and knew it, and you didn't know what to do about it. Again you asked me not to abandon you, and again, helpless about how else not to, I put some money on your table. My cousin said, "He'll run to town and spend it on the girls." And I said, "Well, for God's sake, let's *hope* so, at least."

Roly-poly, old boy, your church music is great, your patriotic songs are great, *you* are great, nobody knows you, but you are great.

Near the end, a few bachelor friends were at your bedside, and one of them, Doc Shotigian said, "Prof, listen to me. Do you understand? What can we get for you now?"

"Girls," you said, and died.

The dark horseman from the hills reached you, and took you God knows where—straight to one of the little hotels on Broadway in Fresno, or to the Paris of Vincent d'Indy's time, or to Great Armenia restored, or to the top of Mt. Ararat.

*Sammy Isaacs:* WE WERE AT THE FRED FINCH
Orphanage together in the Ward for Small Boys in
Oakland, California, in 1911, 1912, 1913, 1914, and
1915, but by now you've forgotten me and everybody else in that strange world and life, which I
suspect you hated even more than I did, for I at
least had my brother there also, as well as my two
sisters, and every once in a while my mother came
over from San Francisco to visit the four of us,
and I remember a picnic we had sitting on grass
on a hill looking down on San Francisco Bay.

You didn't seem to have *anybody* to come
and visit you. Teddy Dolan was also in that ward
with us. I heard that he became a cop in San Fran-

cisco, and sometimes stood at Third and Mission controlling traffic, but I never saw him. What's the good of it? The remote past is past, and good riddance, but then again it never seems to be *entirely* past, so that every now and then I remember two things about us: first, we were friends and spent time together talking, and second, some older boys pushed us into a fight neither of us wanted to get into, but we listened to them, trying our best not to, and clenched our fists and tried to strike each other, but didn't really make it, and began to cry at the same time, not because we had hurt each other but because there was this matter of older people deliberately setting out to make a man believe his friend is in fact his enemy.

I think it had to do with race and religion, but also with several other things. In the first place I didn't know there *was* such a thing as a race, beyond the human one, and even if there happened to be a hundred different races, I couldn't see how that made it necessary for me to fight you, but I was told you were a Jew, and that I was an Armenian, and that I ought to give you a beating, and you were told that you ought to give me a beating—the older boys who had aligned themselves on my side making me believe I would be disgraced if I didn't fight you, while the older boys who had aligned themselves on your side made you feel something of the same sort. The whole thing was bogus and stupid, and as little as we were, and as ignorant, we both sensed that we were being used for the amusement of the others. One likes to have allies and friends, but if their purpose is to belittle life, one isn't sure one ought to have them.

When the fight stopped, suddenly and inconclusively, I was both surprised and glad that all of my friends walked away with all of your friends, leaving us alone to face each other in the truth, and instantly became friends again. Fifty-five years ago it was, and yet it's one of those little experiences of early life that hangs on. As far as I am able to remember, the matter of race or religion didn't come up again between us, for in that place there was really only one other race and religion, that of older people.

Miss Winchester, our matron, a very large woman who was especially overbearing when it was bath day, expected us to present ourselves to her one by one, so she could pick us up and set us down into a tub and see that we soaped all over, so she could pour water over us and wash away the soap, pick us out of the tub, hand us a towel to dry with, and send us back to our clothes. What I felt was, by what right did she pick me up and set me down into the water, with her hard red hands? But she wasn't a bad sort, really, and hardly the worst matron in the world. She just didn't look or smell right, as far as I was concerned. And then to make matters worse, whenever she hollered at one or another of the seven or eight small boys in our ward, she always asked them why they couldn't behave like me, which was really nothing I cared to take pride in at all. I didn't know how to behave in any other way. *Get along* became my purpose in a matter of not much more than one hour after I arrived at that place, because it seemed to me that if I didn't get along a very poor situation would become hopeless, as of course it must have been for the boys in our ward who cried every night the minute the lights were turned off by Miss Winchester.

I listened and I did a lot of thinking. I decided I must be very lucky, because I really didn't want to cry, or didn't need to, and the crying boys either wanted to or had to, I wasn't sure which. It might have been both, but in any case the fact that they cried every night seemed to suggest that the orphanage was even more hateful to them than it was to me. I never teased any of them, and I don't believe you did, either, although there were always two or three boys who every morning said to two or three others, "I heard you bawling last night, you little bawl-baby."

The old maid, Blanche Fulton, spent a lot of time at the orphanage at her own expense, and frequently took all seven or eight of us to Diamond

Canyon or to a park somewhere, which was like getting us out of prison for a while.

I remember one day at a park seeing a lot of small boys who looked as unhappy as we did, and certainly were nowhere as neatly got out as we were, each of us in his own little freshly laundered and starched shirt and clean pants, and suddenly one of these boys shouted to another, "Hey, Pete, come and look at the orphans." Two boys ran up and looked at us, while we looked at them.

The boy who had been called had a very thin head, and speaking almost to myself and certainly meaning no rudeness and totally ignorant of how the word came to my mind, I said, "Pinhead." I must have heard the word from an older boy. But the thing I'm remembering is that I didn't dislike either of the boys, in spite of their rudeness, and I didn't call the boy with the narrow head a name, I simply found that I had said the word and that the boy had heard me and was shocked and hurt.

And then I believed that, since he had believed I had called him a name and was shocked and hurt, misunderstanding, he would fight, and even though the whole thing was a mistake and a misunderstanding, I would fight back, but not the way it had been with you and me when the older boys had tried to provoke us into amusing them a little by hitting each other in the face. I really didn't know why I would fight back, although it seemed to me that they had insisted on it, shouting about us as if we were freaks of some kind, and had come up suddenly, running and skidding, and had stared at us.

They *were* different. They were boys with homes and parents, and freedom to go and come as they pleased, but they were also stupid, and so if the boy with the narrow head wanted to fight, I didn't mind at all, in fact I wished he would.

And then something terrible happened that made me think some more about the whole thing. The poor boy began to cry, and just stood there, didn't turn and go away and cry in private. And his crying hurt me and made me ashamed. This boy, with a home and parents, was just as unhappy as the boys in our ward who cried every night. Now, how could that be? And his crying had me almost crying, because I had said the word that had hurt him, and because I can't make a discovery about the emotions of people without being deeply moved myself, partly by the discovery and partly by their pain and sorrow.

So I said, "I'm sorry, I didn't mean to call you a name."

And then his friend, the other boy, began to chant, "Pinhead, Pinhead, Pinhead Pete," and again I was amazed. They were friends. Why was the other boy, bigger and stronger and with a perfectly head-shaped head, a round head, why was he attacking and hurting his own friend?

So then I said, "Don't call him names." And I clenched my fists, because this whole thing was my fault. I didn't like what was happening because a crazy word had come to my mind and mouth. I wanted the saying of the word not to have been as wrong a thing as it seemed to be getting to be. The other boy took the challenge and said, "I'll call him names all I want. Pinhead, Pinhead, Pinhead Pete."

So I hit him, but not in the face, only on the shoulder. He grabbed my arms and we began to wrestle. The way I felt about what I had started, I'm sure I would have given him a beating if Blanche Fulton hadn't come up and stopped us.

Later, I found the boy with the narrow head and I spoke to him. I think by that time he really believed I hadn't meant to call him a name, and that made me feel better. I had a nickel I had had for a long time. I don't know what I was saving it for, but who knows about saving money? I brought the nickel out of my pocket and held it out to the boy.

"Here," I said.

He took the nickel so quickly that again I was surprised and had to do some more thinking.

Hell, the boy was poor, that's all. He was poorer than me, even. He lived at home with his mother and father, but they were all poor. His clothes were almost rags, his shoes were all worn out, and he looked hungry, even. Just because he was home with his father and mother didn't mean things were better for him than they were for me, or for you, or for any of the other boys in our ward. He seemed to be as much of an orphan as any of us, and if anything a *sadder* one than any of us. Well, how come? That was the question. What makes an orphan?

A few days later I ran away, but I came back after wandering around Diamond Canyon, where there was a rock pool shaded by ferns and oak trees. I went there to see the little silent fish in the water, and to think. They were the most beautiful things I had ever seen, serene in the water, among rocks and shadows. They were alone, too, weren't they? They were so perfect I longed to acquire some of their perfection—first by just looking at them and thinking, and then by reaching into the water, not to hurt them, but to greet them, to let them know I loved them. They waited until my hand moved too near, and then suddenly they moved away, silently, like light. I thought about that, too, and while I didn't like their distrust, I think I understood it. I certainly accepted it. After what seemed a long time I decided to find my way back to the orphanage and not tell anybody I had run away.

When I got back to our dormitory to wash

before supper you said, "Where were you? I thought maybe you ran away."

"No, I just went to Diamond Canyon to look around. I don't want to run away," I said.

I would have told you exactly what had happened, except that I was sure I wouldn't know how, because everybody was always talking about running away, and every one of us believed it was the one thing we lived for. And I knew if I tried to explain what had actually happened, you'd think I was telling a lie.

*Al Devarine:* IT'S THIRTY YEARS SINCE I SAW YOU last, running the elevator in the Mattei Building on J Street, later called Fulton, a building I saw go up in 1919 before my very eyes, when I sold papers across the street on the Kinema Theatre corner.

I really never expected to see a man like you running an elevator, but there you were, almost thirty years old and nothing better to do than go up eight floors, opening and shutting doors, and then down. I thought something must be wrong somewhere, because at Emerson School you were one of the great comics. Your parody of Long-fellow's *Hiawatha* was one of the greatest improvisations I had ever heard, and each time it was different and seemed to be better than the time before. For God's sake, Al, what happened? I felt sure that if anybody would make a way for himself in the world, it would be you, but there you were in the stupid elevator, a total loss, a man in abject ruin.

I didn't want to speak to you. I felt it would be rude. I didn't want to believe it was you. But you recognized me and said my name, so I *had* to say yours. The elevator began to go up, so I had to say four, because that's where Krikor Arakelian's office was. We said the usual things that always get said under such circumstances, but I was glad to get out of the elevator. When I saw my brother playing backgammon with Krikor Arakelian I said, "Do you know who runs the elevator in this building?"

"Al Devarine," my brother said. "When I saw him, I couldn't believe my eyes, either. The funniest kid at Emerson School—the greatest natural comedian of them all."

"What the hell happened?"

"You tell me," my brother said. "Sit down until I win this game, too, and then we'll go visit our grandmother Lucy."

The winemaker said, "What's the hurry? She's an old woman, she'll get a little older, why break up the game?"

I sat for almost an hour, and then my brother said, "I won every game, but what good is it, you don't play for money, Mr. Arakelian. Let's go."

We went out into the hall. The millionaire winemaker decided to go with us, to say hello to the old lady, but also to see if he could get my brother to return to his office and play some more. He pressed the button for the elevator, but suddenly I didn't want to ride down, so I took the stairs and I was down and in the street before my brother and Arakelian came out into the glaring light.

That's all, Al, old friend. What happened, to put you into that elevator? That stupid moving coffin?

What killed you, old pal?

*Samuel L. Clemens:* THE DOG DAYS ARE UPON PARIS. Everything has got the sun upon itself full face. Anybody who goes out to walk sweats and complains to himself.

The whole city is jumping with American travelers, as well as travelers from everywhere else in the world. The streets are crowded with people holding guidebooks and looking up at buildings: Napoleon had a furnished room on the fifth floor up there, to which every evening he took a loaf of bread and a piece of cheese, which he ate while he planned how someday he would take Russia.

Or, in this building in 1747 François Chambertin was born. He later became the lawyer

who unsuccessfully defended Jean-Claude Mar-
chavonne on the charge of having murdered the
concierge of the building, an old maid who was
deaf and dumb.

In and out among the Paris taxis and automobiles move any number of enormous travel
buses, each filled to capacity with passengers from
Germany, Sweden, Denmark, Norway, Italy, Argen-
tina, Brazil, and Mexico.

Everybody travels these days, everybody
takes some kind of grand tour sooner or later,
or once in a lifetime. And right now the travel
season is at its height.

The people in the streets walk from landmark to landmark and refer continuously to the
guidebooks. And they add to the heat already in
the city. Everybody who can't speak French says to
French people at bistros that it's very hot by fan-
ning themselves with guidebooks, or by just standing there drenched in sweat as they sip a coffee.

Yes, everybody still talks about the weather,
and nobody does anything about it, although
sensible travelers get off the streets and go to a
hotel room where they take an afternoon nap,
feeling far from home and happy, and a little
guilty about not being out there looking at the
buildings, churches, squares, statues, monuments,
and whatever else is in the guidebooks.

Another thing people always talk about but

never do anything about is the news. Well, it's bad. It's very bad. The crazy stuff going on every day is crazier than it used to be, and those who are engaged in making the madness tell lies about it every day, and these lies are reported in the papers every day. If they weren't, there wouldn't be very much to read in the papers. It's the same old place in the same old weather, only hotter and worse.

Yes, sir, everybody is still only talking, but maybe that's the best thing possible for this animal.

*Dikran Saroyan:* I NEVER SAW YOU, BUT YOUR SISTER,
my mother, Takoohi, told me about you, and so
did your brother, Aram, and so did your mother,
Lucy, and so did quite a number of other members of the family, or friends or enemies who had
known you, without a doubt the most irritable
man in the family, but at the same time the funniest.

When I was in my early twenties, one of
your cousins, first or second, or once or twice
removed, I don't know which, but at any rate a
Saroyan, the one called Moushegh, at that time in
his late fifties, said, "Dikran's fault was that he was
obsessed by women. Nobody went to the whore-

houses in Chinatown as often as he did, sometimes three times a day. It may not have killed him, but along with his restlessness, impatience, annoyance with everybody, and the touch of T.B. he always had, it certainly helped. He was very funny, but also very rude, obscene in gesture and speech, although I myself enjoyed a pleasant relationship with him."

After thirty years of hearing stories about you I knew what others thought of you, at any rate.

I was three years old when you decided to go back to Bitlis, in 1911, but died on the way, in Constantinople. Nobody has been able to satisfy me as to why you left your wife, although everybody has put forward a theory, or a guess.

Your mother Lucy said, "The poor boy believed he would be restored to health in Bitlis. It was his intention to come back as soon as he was well again."

Your sister Takoohi said, "He was told there was an Armenian doctor in Constantinople who could restore his health, and so he went to see the doctor."

Your brother Aram said, "He didn't like America, he didn't like California, he didn't like Fresno, he was sorry he ever came, so he went back."

But I gathered that each of them didn't

❊  73  ❊

know the real reason and was guessing, or *did* know it and was keeping it to himself for some reason or another, possibly because it was shameful. Nobody said you had syphilis, for instance, but it seems quite likely that it might have been so.

And nobody so much as mentioned that you left an infant son, by name Ara, who was of course my own cousin. I mean, had I known he was somewhere near Fresno, I am sure I would have sought him out, if only to see what sort of a son you had had. You scarcely saw him yourself, and then you were gone.

Finally I did see him—in the Burnett Sanatorium in Fresno, aged seventeen. With me at the time were five or six other cousins, and he said, "Isn't it strange that I am meeting some of my many cousins at this particular time?" And there was no doubt that he knew he was dying. He had a well-shaped head, a narrow face, and very dark intelligent eyes. He had only just graduated at the top of his high-school class and had given the valedictory speech. He certainly looked like one of us, and in his face I believed I saw his strange father.

And then he died, and very nearly all of his relatives on his father's side saw him for the first time, and he was buried.

Your son Ara was one of the best cousins I ever met, and I met him only that one time. He had pride, and something even more difficult to come by—dignity. At that time, with the sudden revelation of what to him must have seemed like a betrayal by his father's entire family, his dignity was terribly moving.

He had never known his father, he had only known a stepfather, but here was his father's kid brother, and five or six sons of his father's three sisters, and he saw that he shared something with all of them, but had something that was his alone: pride, dignity, and death, all mixed together.

All of them looked a little like one another and a little like him, but only he was on his way out —already. It was no joke, but he smiled and laughed at the stories his cousins told about one another, and he didn't permit himself even once to show his annoyance, boredom, or anger, which I was sure he felt, being your son and my cousin, and I imagined how you might have spoken under the same circumstances—how you would have cursed your visitors and told them to get the hell out of your sight.

It happened a long time ago, it has all been forgotten, but to me it remains a terrible puzzle. The best I can do is believe you started to go back to Bitlis, not because you had T.B. or syphilis or both, or because you believed there was a doctor in Constantinople who could restore your health, but because you had to go somewhere to get away from yourself, and the highlands of Bitlis, where you were born, seemed the place to go, whether to live or to die. And your son died of cancer at the age of seventeen for reasons unknown, or for the same reasons you died of whatever you died of when you died—perhaps pride, perhaps arrogance, but possibly contempt for the whole human family, even the Saroyans, even your own son.

*Joe Gould:* DON FREEMAN TOLD ME ONE DAY IN New York he knew a man I ought to meet, Joe Gould.

Well, at the age of fifteen in Fresno one rainy afternoon when I had been working on a vineyard pruning vines and work had been suspended on account of the rain, I went to a bookstore that had a lot of old magazines, and among them I found a copy of *The Dial,* took it home and began to read it from cover to cover. And then suddenly there was some writing by Joe Gould, a fragment of *An Oral History of the World,* although I have seen it referred to as The *Oral History of the World,* as well.

I liked the writing, it was simple, straight, and funny. And I liked the *idea* of an oral history of the world. It was a good idea, and I was glad you had hit upon it.

The next day Don Freeman brought you up to the Hampshire House on Central Park South where I was staying in those days, or he took me to a Gypsy restaurant somewhere in the Village, I forget which, but in any case I met you, and after that you sometimes came up to the Hampshire House and I sometimes visited you in the Village. You were a very small man in very old clothes. You wore a very large beard, stained brown around the mouth, and now and then you removed your false teeth, apparently for comfort, to ease the mouth, and looked at them, and told stories about your adventures in connection with them—losing them, dropping them, having them stepped on, having them stolen while you slept in a Village hall somewhere, and so on.

I was thirty-one or thirty-two at the time, and in the money at last, from the writing and selling of short stories, and from the writing and directing of plays, and you were fifty-one or fifty-two, and very unsuccessful, but always high-spirited and with a lot of stories to tell.

And then with my own money, at my own theater, which was actually the Belasco Theatre on 44th Street, I produced and directed an antiwar play

called *Across the Board on Tomorrow Morning,*
in which Maxwell Bodenheim performed a part
that was no more and no less than the part he performed in the various bars of the Village, where I
had seen him.

Well, it seems he was an old friend of yours
who was an old enemy, and so you came to the
Belasco one afternoon during a rehearsal and you
urged me to throw the bum out and put you in his
place. His poem, "Jazz Music," which he recited in
the saloon near the end of the play, stank, you
said: it was out of date and corny. You would be
glad to recite your "Quack Sonnet" instead, so I
asked you to let me hear it, and it turned out to be
fourteen lines of the word "quack" repeated ten
times to a line.

I thought it was an interesting poem, and I
thought you did it well, standing in the foyer at
the Belasco, but I didn't think it suited the play, so
I said I was sorry but I had hired Bodenheim and I
really couldn't have two poets in one play, both of
them real, both of them famous characters. You
then said you would work free, but for God's sake
throw out Bodenheim, the man was a phony. In
the end, though, Bodenheim stayed in the play, but
the play got bad reviews and had a very short run.
The war had started, it was too late to put on an
antiwar play, and I myself passed the Army physi-
cal at St. Joseph's, taking time out from a rehearsal
to go there by taxi.

And so for the following three years I was away from the theater, and in the Army.

After the War, and after I had been out of the Army for a year or two, Joseph Mitchell phoned me, and so we met at "21" for lunch. He said he was writing a piece for *The New Yorker* about you and had some questions he wanted to ask me.

"What about this history he's writing?" he said.

"From what I've seen of it, I think it's a great work," I said.

"What have you seen?"

"A part of it that came out in *The Dial* many years ago, and stuff Joe Gould carried around in the back pocket of his pants and now and then read aloud to me at the Hampshire House."

"Did you ever see anything resembling a manuscript?"

"No, Joe Gould said he had a lot of it in cardboard boxes stashed here and there in the Village. Soon after I first met him, I spoke about Joe Gould to three publishers, and I set up appointments for him, but he either broke them or forgot them. Or he phoned and asked for an advance, but didn't have a manuscript to show the publisher. I get the impression Joe isn't sure he wants his history to be published."

About a year later the piece Joseph Mitchell

wrote about Joe Gould came out in *The New Yorker,* and of course I read it.

And then you disappeared.

I asked Don Freeman about you and he said you were ill, in a home somewhere.

A few years later I read in *The New York Times* that you had died.

And five or six years after that Joseph Mitchell brought out a whole book about Joe Gould in which he gave the matter of *An Oral History of the World* a very careful and thorough examination. His conclusion was that you never wrote anything more than the stuff that came out in *The Dial* and the few fragments you kept in the back pocket of your pants. You *talked* about the *History*. You made a legend of yourself, of being at work all the time on a great book, but you never actually saw the thing through.

Well, I'll tell you what I'm going to do, Joe. One of these days I'm going to write *Joe Gould's Oral History of the World* myself. I think I know what you had in mind, and I think I can get it into writing as well as any other American writer who knew you.

*Miss Carmichael, Miss Thompson, Miss Brock-
ington, Miss Clifford, Miss Chambers:* I SAW YOU
at Emerson School in Fresno fifty years ago every
schoolday for four or five years, and am only lately
beginning to forget, but before I do, before the
failure of memory is total, before even your names
become difficult or even impossible to remember,
let me see if I can tell you how I felt then about
you and how I feel now, for it is teachers who at
the beginning of the awakening of the mind drive
a man to himself, or away—a very small and green
man, not at all sure what the trouble is everywhere, or what he is to do about it.

Emerson School was two buildings, each

precisely square, each with two floors. Before my arrival there from 2226 San Benito Avenue, only half a block from the southeast edge of the school-grounds, many others had gone to the school, a few of them in my own family, and the majority of them Armenians, since the school was in the heart of what used to be known as Armenian Town, but has since become Mexican and Negro town, the Armenians having long since prospered and moved to better neighborhoods, excepting a few old widows or widowers who still occupy the houses they occupied when I was seven or eight years old. They still have grapevines in their backyards, and peach and apricot trees. But the once-favored mulberry trees have all been uprooted, and only a few of the old almond and walnut trees remain standing. But their time is limited, too.

No one is going to be unsympathetic about the hard work it must have been for you to manage classrooms full of Armenian boys and girls, as well as a number of Syrians, Assyrians, Slavonians, Portuguese, Irish, and what we used to call Americans. The Italians, Greeks, and Russians (who were actually Germans who had gone to Russia for religious freedom, and from Russia had come to California), and the Mexicans, the Chinese, and the Japanese, made their homes across the Southern Pacific tracks on the west side, and went to Columbia School. They formed another world, but we all met in the town and knew one another at least by sight.

The teachers at Columbia also had very hard work to do. The kids of immigrants aren't easy to manage, for they are quickly made aware of a number of attitudes held by others about them, mainly that they are not the equal of Americans, or at any rate not the equal of those Americans who are not poor, and in reply to these unfriendly and frequently rude attitudes these kids behaved in a manner suited to the disadvantages they lived under.

First, there was a nickname for each group that amounted to an insult, not so much because of the nickname itself, but for the contempt with which it was frequently flung at a member of the group not only by angered members of other groups, but also by adults and teachers themselves. It was so bad that simply to refer to a boy by his nationality, as an Armenian, for instance, became the equivalent of an expression of contempt and, of course, an insult. And so it was with the boys and girls whose parents were Italians or Russians, and so on. It was soon so undesirable to be what you were that many boys and girls wished to God they were something else, and even tried to pretend that they were actually not Armenian, for instance, but Persian. Or they couldn't wait to get out of school, and out of town, so that they could forget what an unfortunate thing it was to be who they were.

Noticing all this, I found it impossible not to expose the absurdity of it, which in turn got me into a lot of trouble. I was who I was, and I refused to accept any theory that what I was was less than what anybody else was, in Fresno or anywhere else. I refused to accept anybody's disrespectful attitude toward me on the basis of my nationality. On any other account anybody could be as disrespectful as he might care to be. That was his business. My business was not to be driven afield from myself, because that was all I had to work with, and I had in mind working in my own way with everything I had.

Some of you were decent and reasonable, but one of you was so limited in mind and spirit that your hatred for almost everybody you were supposed to teach was open and constant, especially for me, because of what you considered my arrogance, my refusal to accept anything you said that I considered unwarranted, my boredom with your limitations, and my acting up, as you put it. Miss Clifford, whoever you are these days, wherever you may be, whatever you may think about anything at all, I despised you then and I cannot now say I am sorry I did. I had no choice. You were despicable, dishonest, rude, stupid, hostile, and unfit to teach anybody anything. You marked me as your personal enemy and started every day with sarcasm about my appearance, my clothing, my manners, my intelligence, and my impatience with your inability to get your work organized or to perform it effectively. And you never learned that any sarcasm from you would be answered in kind by me.

Without intending to do so, you taught me to learn how to suffer fools, which is something every man must learn, and the sooner the better. I thank you for *that*, at any rate.

Miss Brockington, thin, austere, orderly, prim, older than the other teachers, and said to have a wooden leg, I respected you for the simple reason that you did not hold against me either my nationality or my personality, but on the contrary struggled decently with each, impelling me in return to struggle with them on your behalf. A dozen times a day I resisted an opportunity, or an almost overpowering impulse, to point out to you how mistaken you were about something or other, because decent and simple courtesy must be respected in another, however mistaken he may be. I insisted on keeping to myself your misconceptions about such things as whom to emulate in the world and what to aspire to in life. Your heroes were invariably frauds, and the ultimate goal you identified for all of us was to find a job and keep it. A fair enough goal in many ways, but much too limited and belittling to most of us.

Miss Chambers, I may as well confess I fell in love with you, if you can understand such a thing and if I can explain how it may have happened. To begin with, you were a woman of beauty, perhaps twenty-five years of age to my eight or nine, your voice was good to hear, you had earnestness, dignity, and a kind of sorrow I considered to be the consequence of homeless love. There was a faint scent of flowers about you at all times, as well as a scent of womanhood. I wanted to have you and to take away in myself something that was yours alone, that no other woman had. And I thought you encouraged me by smiling now and then about something I had just said, which you found unexpected. This smile seemed to me a thing of great privacy, and any day in which your smile reached me I considered a day of good fortune. It gave me a feeling of success and importance, as a man comes to have in possessing a woman.

This good feeling stayed with me as I sold papers after school, as I hollered headlines, and as I went home to supper and comedy and bed and sleep. It was in sleep one night that I saw the smile again, heightened in meaning as all things are in sleep, and ever afterward loved you with all of my being, and in a sense still do.

❋ 87 ❋

## WILLIAM SAROYAN

Miss Carmichael, I owe you a great deal for keeping me in after school one day, not as punishment, but to tell me that I must promise to go to college, that you knew I was somebody. I had always gathered that I was, but very few others before you had even so much as hinted that this was so, and then you brought it home to me openly, compelling me to be concerned about the responsibility involved. I thank you for this. I didn't go to college, but that's beside the point, or rather I went in my own way, which I presume is what you meant, in any case. Your brother had been killed in France in the War, as you told the whole class one morning, and ever afterward there was a tenderness, patience, sympathy, and sorrow in you that I found terribly moving.

And finally Miss Thompson. When I presented myself to you by appointment an hour before classes one day, so that you might give me a special test of some kind, you put a drawing of a domestic scene before me and asked me to say the things the scene meant to me. I said so many things you finally stopped jotting them down and took the picture away, so that we might move along to other parts of the test. You were unable to conceal your surprise about the things I found in the picture, and I myself was a little surprised by the variety of things it was impossible for me not to see. Apparently nobody else who had taken the test had seen so much in the picture, and this seemed to you to mean something, because the rest of that day you kept sending for me, so that I might be seen by somebody unknown to me who was in your office, and after that day every teacher looked at me in a new way, and I knew I was now known as somebody who must be noticed.

In short, you brought me the first taste of fame I ever experienced. Even poor Miss sharp-nosed Clifford hated me in a new and more important way.

Now, since those days at Emerson School, I have looked into the whole business of teaching, of schools, of systems of education, and I am sorry to say I can find nothing of any real value that makes one system better than another, or more certain to impel growth in a new man, although no system I have ever heard about, or read about, might be said to be inferior to the system at Emerson School, or the Fresno Public School System. I have read Tolstoy's theories about teaching and schools, and about the Montessori System, and about the Permissive System, and about a great many other systems, and while the intentions of all of them are excellent, one is never sure the intentions are ever fulfilled. So that I am left with the conclusion that everybody acquires the benefits he needs or is entitled to *in spite of,* and not on account of, the educational system involved.

## WILLIAM SAROYAN

Excepting the teaching of such skills as medicine and engineering, for instance, a man learns what he needs not from a system of teaching, but from the teachers themselves, in their own persons, and not by their methods or their rules.

A man learns from the human race itself, in short, and the very best that I ever learned was at home, or in the streets, or at the various jobs I held before I became twenty. School was mainly a waste of my valuable time, after I had learned to read and write.

*Honoré de Balzac:* THIS IS YOUR CITY, AND WHO CAN
pretend it isn't one of the most majestic ever to
appear upon the face of the earth? It is a city of
illumination, fountains, great squares, monuments,
broad boulevards, parks, and trees. It has great
museums, libraries, schools, art galleries, and con-
cert halls. In short, a city of enlightenment, cul-
ture, awareness, intelligence, wit, and beauty.

And yet one almost never believes any of
the people who are in the streets, or anybody one
happens to meet anywhere else, is especially en-
lightened, cultured, aware, intelligent, amusing, or
beautiful.

Last night at the Aviation Club on the

Avenue des Champs Élysées, for instance, upstairs at number 104, there they were again: the Corsican gambling-house workers, and the stiff executives with their keen knowledge of human weakness.

And there were the players, God help them, and there was I, with them. All of us gone mad.

It is a beautiful city, but when a man gambles and drinks and smokes all night, he really can't be said to be *in* the city, although at six this morning when I came walking down rue Notre-Dame-de-Lorette from Pigalle, I really *was* in Paris, and stopping to take a piss I thought it was a magnificent thing, how God made the human body, and put in all of its pipes and passages, containers, filters, purifiers, distilleries, and all the rest of it. I thanked Him for Paris, and for private plumbing.

It's not my city, but early this morning, coming home, I sang *How great Thou art*. And climbed five flights of stairs, and flung myself upon my bed, and slept and woke up and drank water, and slept some more, and woke up, and drank some more water, because if you drink whiskey for twelve hours you've got to put water on the fire to keep it from burning you up.

And then at last I slept and dreamed heaven, and got up and went out and walked, and looked at your city again and your people, Balzac, and each of them was just fine. Each of them was a strange little faraway city himself.

*Sam Catanzaro:* WHEN I WORE THE BLUE JACKET
of the uniform for messengers of the Postal Telegraph Company in Fresno in 1921, 1922, and 1923,
you came out from Pittsburgh to buy carloads of
grapes for your produce house. During the three
years that I was a messenger we became friends—
without any exchange of words, although one year
when I answered a call from your office you said,
"You've grown a lot since last summer." I had, of
course, but I hadn't noticed.

You frequently had a lot of cars rolling that
you wanted diverted from one destination to another, and you told the manager of the telegraph
office that you would prefer to have me take the di-

version forms from your office to the Santa Fe or the Southern Pacific because I moved quickly and could be trusted—not that any of the other seven messengers couldn't be, or that there was any temptation of any kind involved. Even so, when J. D. Tomlinson said you wanted me to look after the diversion forms for you, I felt proud and grateful. It meant that my job was even more assured than it was in any case, since from the beginning I had taken it upon myself to be the fastest messenger in the office or, for that matter, in the city. Even R. L. Hunter, the manager of the Western Union office, knew I was faster than any of his eleven or twelve messengers, and he several times told my brother Henry I could have a job at his office any time I cared to make a change, but I never took him up. My brother went to work for Postal Telegraph first, and a month later I followed him. That office was my home in the business world.

I suppose you were in your early thirties in those days, a man of medium height but seeming large, with a touch of darkness about your face, along with the thick black hair. So that now, forty-five years later, you are nearly eighty, and your kids have got kids and their kids have got kids.

Before going home to Pittsburgh one December you said, "I'll see you next summer. In the meantime, here's a little gift." And you handed me an envelope in which I found a brand-new five-dollar bill. Well, of course I had only done my work, for which you had been fully charged by the telegraph company and for which I had been fully paid: fifteen dollars a week. You were not obliged to pay me anything extra or to give me a gift, but you did so. I reasoned that you suspected I could always use a little extra money and that in passing along a little to me you were letting me know you believed I ought to be encouraged in whatever it might be that was at the back of my head. It was writing, of course, although nobody knew this.

I took the gift of five dollars to mean that you did know, or that you suspected something of the sort, and wanted me to know that whatever it was, you wished me luck.

For my part, I wished the same to you, for I knew that the buying and selling of carloads of grapes was risky business. I had seen others suddenly go broke, and quit, or be reduced to taking employment with other houses. I have frequently wondered how things have gone with you and with the Catanzaro people in the grape-buying-and-selling business, and I have always believed they have gone quite well, because it seemed to me that they *must*. But who knows? The most decent people in the business world, the most deserving, can have a run of bad luck and find themselves in a bad way. I saw it happen during three years of being a messenger, to a lot of different people, some good, some bad, some a mixture of both—that is, good in good times, bad in bad. But I never saw an out-and-out crook—liar and cheater—who ever made it really good, or ever amounted to anything worth noticing, even after a very lucky season. He was still a crook, and his success didn't improve matters any.

I have tried to pass along your kindness.

*Vahan Minasian:* WHEN I THINK OF ALL THE TIME that has gone by since our last meeting I can scarcely believe that it is myself who is still here, and still for all the world as much who he had been as who he is, so that remembering our first important meeting I am still unable not to be astonished by your words, and grateful for them.

I paid a silver dollar in 1917 for a nickel-plated badge every boy who sold *The Fresno Evening Herald* was obliged to buy and wear, a badge that resembled a cop's badge but really didn't mean anything. It was something I bought with reluctance and a feeling of being gypped. It had several engraved words on it, and a number, but I can only guess that the words said, *The Fresno Evening Herald,* Newsboy Number 8, although it might have been another number, as the badges were sold and handed out on the basis of first come, first served. I pinned the badge to my wool shirt, bought at the Army surplus store called Western Sales. I took my papers and ran to town. In those days I had no corner, I sold wherever I could, moving all the time. Now and then I noticed the badge, but after a while I forgot all about it.

When I had sold all of my papers, twenty, for a profit of half a dollar, and was ready to walk home and have supper, I noticed that the badge was gone.

Well, it must have fallen somewhere, so instead of going home, I began to go over the course I had followed for two or three hours. I looked for the badge, but I didn't find it. I covered the course again, and I thought, "Well, if I don't find my badge, maybe I'll find somebody else's, because if I could lose mine, somebody else could lose his, but if I don't find a badge, maybe I'll find something else."

I certainly felt I ought to find something, because a dollar was a lot of money, and any kind of loss in those days seemed to me a very unfortunate thing. I looked all over town either for the badge I had lost or for the badge somebody else had lost, or for something else somebody had lost. I even left the course I had followed and began to look everywhere.

I looked for a long time and found nothing —not a penny, not a nail, not a button. And this made me angry. I had worked hard to earn half a dollar, and then I had worked even harder trying to find the lost badge, or something else, and I had found nothing. I was hungry, thirsty, tired, and frustrated, although the very meaning of such a word was beyond me in those days. I was simply defeated, and I hated being defeated.

When I got home, my mother saw that something was the matter, so I told her what had happened, and she just looked at me and put in front of me a big bowl of grapeleaves stuffed with meat and rice. As hungry as I was, I couldn't eat. When I got up from the table my mother said, "What's the matter?"

"I've got to go back to town and find my badge."

"But you've already looked."

"I'm going to look until I find it."

I ran back to town and again I looked everywhere, growing angrier all the time, but again I found nothing.

I went home very slowly, dead tired, but didn't go inside. Instead, I sat on the steps of the front porch, cursing my luck, trying to understand how and why it had happened, and why I hadn't been able to find the badge after looking for it so carefully.

You came up L Street from your house, and then came down San Benito, my uncle, married to my mother's sister, the father of my cousins Roxie, Zav, Helen, Archie, Kirk, and Stella. I really felt ashamed to be seen by anybody at a time like that, but I was too tired to get up and run to the backyard, and so you saw me, with my face all hungry and angry.

"What is it?" you said. "Tell me."

You were the first adult member of my own family who spoke to me as if I were an equal, and so I told you. I told you exactly what had happened, and how it had happened, and that's when you surprised me.

"Oh, is *that* what it is?" you said. "A badge that cost a dollar? Paid for and immediately lost? That is nothing. May your soul stay alive."

And suddenly everything was all right.

I had still lost a badge, I had still lost a dollar, but now, because of what you had said and the way you had said it, I knew that what had happened was nothing, what had been lost was nothing, the important thing was myself, and the staying alive, as you put it, of my soul.

Nobody has ever said anything more meaningful or useful to me.

A few years later you were gone, having taken off when you were about the same age as my father, thirty-six.

And now, even though I'm twenty years older than you, and twenty years older than my father, I don't know what to make of all the time that's gone by and of all the things that have happened, that nevertheless have left me still abroad in the streets, not only of Fresno but of the world, not necessarily looking for something lost, or something to be found, but just being there, still going and coming, and still looking.

*Geoffrey Faber:* IT WAS IN MAY OF THE YEAR 1935
that I went to 24 Russell Square in London to
meet the publisher of my first book, arriving at
teatime and sharing with a variety of nice people
my first experience of both the British and their
tradition of afternoon tea. Mr. Eliot was up at
Oxford at the moment, and so I missed him, and
do you know, except for a luncheon arranged at the
Connaught by a lady in 1944, I never saw him,
although he once sent me a short, typed letter about
a story I had written during my first travels in
Russia, a story called "The Black Tartars," a letter
which did not seem to require an answer. In any
case, I didn't answer it, for he said he had found
something or other in the story especially interest-

ing, perhaps the matter of the language of the Black Tartars, which was always the language of the people among whom they lived. At tea was Mr. Frank Morley, brother of the American writer Christopher Morley and of the American scholar and college president Felix Morley. Also present was Mr. Morley Kennerley, son of the publisher Mitchell Kennerley, an American, as I understood it, who had gone to London to continue publishing. I was idly struck by the several Morleys on the scene, but didn't ask anybody if Kennerley's given name had been the consequence of his father having known and published Christopher Morley. There were half a dozen bird-voiced rather sweet and helpful secretaries at tea, and although I hadn't really wanted any, or any of the little cakes and little pieces of buttered bread, I had some of each.

It was an exciting time. I had just arrived in London on the *Berengaria,* on my first visit to Europe, my first pilgrimage to the old country. (It wasn't the *Berengaria,* it was its sister ship, but for a moment the name has fled my memory: I went *back* on the *Berengaria.* In any case they were both enormous ships, and I rode third class both ways, which was still to me the most astonishing and magnificent luxury I had ever dreamed I would ever know, or want.—*Acquitania, that* was the ship I went over on.)

I was traveling on money earned as a writer, which in itself was a personal triumph for me, for it had long seemed more likely that even if I made writing my lifework I might be something less than poor, as it was with the writers, some of them great, who did their writing in the Armenian language (because it *was* their language, and not because many of them couldn't write in French, German, Italian, and even in English).

My first book had actually earned money for me. And it seemed quite likely that my writing in the future would also earn money for me. In any case, the moment I knew the cost of going to Europe, and from there to Russia, and on to the capital of Armenia, Erivan, I decided to go—to raise the money and go, for I had wanted to be near where my father had been before he had traveled to America, and on to California, and had died.

I had a noisy, nervous, exuberant, confident, swift way about me, apparently inherited from the maternal side of my line, as against the melancholy and courteous strain of the paternal side.

It would be easy, perhaps it would be unavoidable, for people to look at one another in my presence, expressing silently their disbelief or their amusement. I myself knew this, and wanted to temper my behavior, but I couldn't, it always got away from me, it couldn't be helped, I invariably shouted, told funny stories very swiftly, roared with laughter, changed pace to notice that a secretary looked like a red rose, and then for an instant fell to soft melancholic speech about somebody

I had seen earlier in the day, followed instantly by more shouting, another story, and a third cup of tea.

During that memorable visit, which altogether well under an hour in duration, I remember feeling, "They like me, it must be that I am really a good writer, and they don't mind that I am making so much noise," but at the same time also feeling, "This is terrible, I've got to straighten out, quiet down, stop acting like the greatest new American writer who ever reached London."

In short, I felt both pleased with myself and annoyed, but there was really nothing I could do.

But I have never permitted myself to overstay a visit anywhere, and I soon insisted I must say thanks very much and go. Before I left the premises you asked me to go with you to your office, and there I did in fact quiet down as we chatted a moment. You wanted to know what my itinerary was, and I told you, and then you looked among your books and presented me with two, which I still have and deeply cherish: *Early One Morning*, a collection of writings by children, edited and with an introduction and comments by Walter de la Mare: a book I enjoyed during my travels and ever afterward.

Of the second book you said, "This is a rather strange book, about mysticism in India, with an introduction by Yeats, who is fascinated by such things. You may enjoy it on your travels." I read the book almost immediately, certainly before

I had even reached Russia, and what I remember most vividly about it appears to have been the belief somebody had that there were holy men who, standing upon a very large rock at the bottom of a great mountain, would find themselves still upon the rock but now at the top of the mountain— transported because of some sort of purification of the spirit, and some sort of incredible concentration and faith, and I may say that, like Mr. Yeats in his introduction, I saw no reason to disbelieve; I only saw the need to try to understand what had happened, how much had actually happened, how much had been imagined, and so on. I don't even remember the name of the book, but I liked the contrast between the two books: the very straight, beautiful, and often brilliant writing of children, and the very complex writing of adult mystics, with a respectful introduction by one of the greatest poets of our world.

I always felt lucky to have my works brought out in London by your firm, with your name upon the books not once but twice, although I learned during my first visit that there was in fact only one Faber—yourself.

When you died a few years ago I lost a friend, and I felt great sorrow. Having my books published by Faber & Faber for almost thirty years was the best thing of its kind that ever happened to me.

*Robert McAlmon:* LATELY IN THIS TOWN, PARIS, in July of the year 1967, I have been reading about you in a number of books about the 1920s, Americans in Paris in the 1920s, the writers, the would-be writers, the characters, and the publishers of little magazines. And I have been trying to read around in a paperback book of yours called *A Hasty Bunch,* undated, but apparently brought out sometime in the twenties by Darantière, in Dijon, who did quite a bit of printing or publishing for Americans in those days.

This wandering through the years in the books I have lying around at 74 rue Taitbout is probably the consequence of a virus, and the running of a slight fever. Mr. T. S. Eliot, at lunch in 1944, in London, told me he found it necessary to write whenever he had a slight fever. Well, of course, there *is* a condition of the heightened in almost all writing, whether from a slight fever or from concentration and from the intention of getting the most out of the material involved, but *reading* is another thing, and I seldom read until I have finished my work for the day, in spite of the virus (not on account of it).

Most of the people I have been reading about I have met, but I never knew any of them during the 1920s, I met them years later when things had settled down. In 1920 I was twelve years old, in Fresno. In 1926 I was eighteen and in the California National Guard, having enlisted from hunger in Los Angeles, from whence I had gone to Monterey for two weeks, at a dollar a day.

In 1928, just before I turned twenty, I was in New York for the first time, but wherever I went there was the simple basic problem of earning my way, which I did by finding a job, invariably at work that had no connection with writing or publishing.

It was not until 1935 that I reached Paris for the first time, but I hadn't come to stay, I was on my way to as much of Europe as I could possibly see on the first money I had earned as a writer.

I was back in Paris again in 1939, because I

wanted to see Europe before the start of the War, which I knew could no longer be avoided.

I never went where writers went—there *were* no writers in Fresno. I saw none during the 1926 visit to Los Angeles. In New York in 1928 I visited Greenwich Village almost every day, but only because very near there was where I worked for the Postal Telegraph Company as a clerk in a small office in the wholesale produce district, on Warren Street. And when I went back to California and settled down in San Francisco early in 1929, I still knew no writers.

And yet somehow in July of 1939, precisely twenty-eight years ago, I went into a bookshop in Paris somewhere, and somebody in the bookshop recognized me and suggested that I must meet Mr. James Joyce. She telephoned him, and he and I spoke on the phone—that is to say, I told him my name, Mr. Joyce told me I was mispronouncing my name, I explained that the pronunciation was a concession to the American limitations of speech, and he suggested I might visit him three days later at half-past two in the afternoon.

I never met Joyce. The following day I went to London, and a few days later to Dublin, and then back to New York, and from there back to San Francisco, to do some more writing—a new play called *Sweeney in the Trees,* a title generously given to me by the great writer Flann O'Brien, of

Dublin, properly Brian O'Nolan, but also famous for his writing of a column in the *Irish Times* under the name of Myles Na gCopaleen. I also wrote an absurd play called *Elmer and Lily,* long before the Theater of the Absurd came to be famous. As well as a number of short stories. And then I flew back to New York to direct my second play, *The Time of Your Life.*

Well, it turns out that the bookshop I had wandered into in Paris, in July of 1939, was Shakespeare and Company, and the lady who had telephoned James Joyce was Sylvia Beach, who first published *Ulysses.* I realized all this last night as I read around in her book entitled *Shakespeare and Company,* published in London by Faber & Faber in 1960. I moved quickly in those days, and people and events unavoidably got lost in the shuffle or at any rate got all entangled in a way that might easily never be untangled. In this delightful book by Miss Beach there is much about you in Paris in the days when Miss Beach first opened her shop. You were from Nebraska, you spoke with a twang of some sort, you knew everybody, you paid for everything, and besides being well-liked, you not only did poems and short stories, you founded the Contact Press and published the first work, or nearly the first, of your friend Ernest Hemingway, as well as the work of many other Americans.

### Robert McAlmon

Two years ago I was surprised and delighted to find your book *A Hasty Bunch* in a bargain box outside a small bookstore in this part of Paris. I paid fifty centimes for it, brought it home, and immediately began to read around in it—because I had never before read any of your short stories, but mainly because I remembered your arrival by taxi in San Francisco at the door of 348 Carl Street, late one afternoon in 1937, and after a short visit in the small room in which I worked, we took a taxi to Izzy's on Pacific Street, because that was where I used to do my drinking in those days.

Well, now, how old were you in 1937? I was twenty-nine, so perhaps you were ten years older, but at any rate the twenties in Paris had long since gone, you had had a few to drink before you had arrived by taxi, you looked a little worn and weary but also keyed-up, and during the ride to Izzy's you talked steadily about life among the American writers in Paris in the twenties.

I had read around in your autobiographical book called *Being Geniuses Together*, but that was a chronicle, not art, as I expected the stories in *A Hasty Bunch* to be. It's a very nicely printed book, and just opening it anywhere at random, one has the feeling that the writing must be good, must be writing, must be literature, must be art, but it isn't, not even accidentally here and there, once or twice.

Well, this is still Paris, it's the other side of

❁ III ❁

town, it's 1967, everything has happened to every-body that had to happen, and I'm about to start my sixtieth year, so I find it a little sad that when it was your turn to do your work, you didn't have it. Plagued by a virus, running a little fever, it would have been great that the keyed-up gossip in the taxi in San Francisco almost thirty years ago had, ten years earlier, done some work that I might instantly recognize as true, and cherish, and be grateful for.

*Lawrence Colt:* WELL, IT WAS FROM RIGHT NEAR here in Paris that we took the jeep to Luxembourg and Germany, stopping en route at Verdun overnight. And stopping here and there in half-ruined villages where little kids came running to beg for cigarettes, which we gave them, in January of 1945, better than twenty-two years ago, Pete Argyll the Indian from somewhere in New Mexico driving, yourself a West Point man from somewhere in New England, and I, a Californian, aged thirty-seven, a private. Pete was a Master Sergeant, about twenty-seven, and you were fifty-five or so, a full Colonel, not a wartime one.

As you may remember, I had written a novel

called *The Adventures of Wesley Jackson* in a deal with the Office of War Information and the Army for an airplane ride from London to New York to visit my wife and young son, but after I had kept my part of the bargain, the OWI, the Army, and the Government welshed. They went dead on me, and the bargain turned out to be a dirty trick.

Now, there were quite a few other soldiers in our outfit who flew from London to New York several times for pleasant visits with their mothers, fathers, brothers, sisters, and friends. The way they worked it was to have a Hollywood Colonel take them along when he decided he wanted to break the monotony by a visit to New York.

One day one of these Colonels tripped and fell when he got out of a jeep, and put in for a Purple Heart—and got it.

There was a big Hollywood writer who had become a big Army Colonel, and somehow he got hold of a copy of the manuscript of *The Adventures of Wesley Jackson*. He sent in a report saying that the Army should not permit the novel to be published and, furthermore, that I ought to be shot.

I had never been able to conceal my contempt for his writing, and he in turn tried several times to have me court-martialed in London, but on each occasion you had a talk with him, and so I was not put on trial for something or other—for not being respectful of his writing, I presume.

Now, he probably wasn't a bad sort at all, just careful and clever.

A few years after the end of the War and after he had gone back to Hollywood and the writing of more scenarios, he died, but when I read about it in *Variety* I must confess I wasn't even a little sorry.

How or why he died I have no idea. There were others like him, perhaps more subtle, and I remember that you were especially bedeviled by the one who actually made Brigadier General, flew to Russia, turned in all kinds of reports, and soon after the War was in *Variety* in connection with a big distributing deal he had made with Moscow for the showing of some films he owned or in which he had an interest. And then only a few years later *Variety* reported that he had died, too.

And there were several others of that kind, and they also died.

Well, of course everybody dies, everybody is always dying, so there isn't much point in my talking about that aspect of the matter. So far I haven't read that you have died, but then you're not a *Variety* character, and it may even be that your death would not be news anywhere, except perhaps in your own home town, or in a West Point newspaper or alumni magazine.

But I hope you are still alive and that all goes well with you, because one afternoon when you asked me to your office, before we took the jeep ride I'm remembering, I gave you a bad time.

Your secretary, a grown woman, tried to cut in several times, tried to get me out of there, but you wouldn't have it, and this made me realize that perhaps I was speaking *for* you, too, another man in the Army who was having a bad time.

The upshot of the whole thing was that you were sorry, but you *knew* you couldn't make the Army keep its part of the bargain with me, because you had already tried to do so. I would have to resign myself to waiting out the rest of the War. I thanked you, apologized, and went out to walk the streets of Paris.

One by one the Hollywood characters arrived back in Paris from Christmas and New Year visits in New York, and the old game was on again.

I think one of the main reasons you wanted to take the jeep to Verdun, Luxembourg, and Germany was to get away for a while from the refreshed, returned heroes.

It was a long time ago, a lot of history and a lot of new cleverness has happened in the meantime, and a lot of people of all kinds have fallen by the wayside, always having known that they would. I hope you're still on your feet, though.

*Yeghishe Charentz:* WE MET AT YOUR HOTEL, THE
Metropole on Red Square, in Moscow, in June
of the year 1935, when I was not yet twenty-seven
years old, and you were perhaps thirty-seven, a
small wiry man with a great hawk nose, dark rest-
less eyes that nevertheless had patience and humor,
and a deep warm voice, the greatest poet of Armenia.

Well, now, it's thirty-two years later.

In 1960 I heard that you were imprisoned
in Erivan in 1937, two years after our meeting. The
cocaine you had for so long lived by had been
withdrawn, and for that reason and for surely other
reasons not known to other people, or if known

not broadcast, you ended your life, supposedly by
ramming your head upon the stone wall of your
prison cell. This is a kind of suicide that seems impossible to achieve, but that does not mean that it
*is* impossible, or that you died in some other manner. I don't know. In Erivan in 1960 I was told you
had managed the matter in the manner I have de-
scribed.

Charentz, my friend, what's the matter with
us? Not poets, not writers. What's the matter with
Armenians? Or is that whole thing a fantasy of
some kind, and Armenians are not Armenians,
each of them is only who he is and that's the end
of it? Is it possible we have gone through all that
history in ignorance, not about ourselves alone,
but about everybody, about all nationalities, all
peoples, all tribes—ethnic, as everybody keeps saying in America these days, geographical, political,
religious, economic, industrial, philosophical, and
so on and so forth endlessly—telling ourselves and
everybody else, "We are Armenians and don't ever
forget it."

And somebody else puts forward his message, "We are Abkhazes, and don't ever forget it."
How could I forget it? I didn't know there *was*
such a people until I met a writer in Moscow in
1960 who told me he was an Abkhaz. You couldn't
have wanted to meet a nicer guy. What's more, he
looked like a member of my own family. But that's

not all. In Erivan I met some Kurdish writers, and they were all decent, sincere, courteous, and more often than not isolated and lonely. In Turkey I met Turkish writers, and it was the same with them. All decent men, good men, not especially good writers perhaps, but let the critics or time concern itself with that, it's none of my business. In Israel I met Israeli writers, all kinds of decent men writing in the Hebrew language. In America I met writers who were Jews from Russia and Poland, Hungary and Brooklyn, and they were all writing in English, and they were not only decent but also funny, and like members of my own immediate family.

You wrote a poem when you were a very young man, "My Armenia," which Armenians all over the world read and weep, and recite and weep, and teach their kids to read and weep. I have heard it recited two or three dozen times and have scarcely been able not to weep, not so much from having met you, from having stood in your presence, from having spoken with you, and from having noticed your isolation, loneliness, comedy, and despair, but from the simple majesty of your usage of the Armenian language, from the love in your usage of the language of the rocky land, from the anger about our small place being in the middle of the highway of history, and the refusal of all of us to be dislodged.

What did you mean by *your* Armenia? The words are clear enough that you meant *that* place and *those* people, but what did you really mean? Most Armenians, like most other people—Abkhazes, Kurds, Turks, Israelis, American Jews, Italians, Germans, English, Scots, Irish, French, Greeks, Spanish—are terrible bores, crooks, connivers, conspirators, cheaters, liars, opportunists, and all-around sons of bitches. I have them in my own family, and they amaze me. My mouth falls open in confusion and speechlessness, but I still insist on trying at least to understand them even after it is no longer possible to respect them. Every piece of land on the face of the earth is beautiful, not just the land which is Armenia. So what did you mean? Were you actually talking about something else? Is it not possible that your Armenian might have the same meaning to another man? Might he not be anybody, of any family? And what you said of Armenia, might it not have been said, might it not now be said, of any place on earth?

What's the cocaine for, Charentz? What's the ramming of the head on the stone wall for?

Listen, I have not forgotten what you said when my appointment to visit Maxim Gorky with you was canceled because of what I had written at the request of a number of Russians in Moscow, about my impressions of Armenia, of Russia, but more particularly about people, about human life under Communism. They asked for it, and I wrote it. I wrote it free of charge and they even kept the manuscript. I never make carbon copies, so they have the only copy, or they destroyed it, or lost it. I don't have it, and therefore am unable to study the absurdity of my trying with all my heart to write honestly.

You said, "My boy, you must try to be a little more clever than that. Say yes, and spit in their eye."

In other words, "Avoid trouble, keep the truth to yourself. This is not the time or place for it."

And instantly I felt how right you were.

Well, then, Charentz, why didn't *you* say yes, and spit in their eye? The truth is coming out now little by little, and it isn't hurting Communism, or Russia, or Armenia, or people, or anything else—it's *helping*. Why aren't you here to notice this for yourself?

Charentz, my boy, in Moscow you were my father, but now it's different, and I am old, older than I once believed I would ever be, but I am also still young, and as you see still writing, so listen again:

Your little daughter in your room in Moscow in 1935, to whom you were feeding expensive pastry at a time when bread was hard to come by, because you were a great writer and entitled to the best of everything, feeding the beautiful little girl food as wrong for her as cocaine was for you—I saw her in Erivan in 1960, and in her arms was her little son, also named Yeghishe Charentz.

I saw them both, my dear friend and countryman, and they were beautiful.

There you were again in your mother's arms. And there was your Armenia, and your Armenian people.

"My sun-flavored Armenia," you said in your poem, which is impossible to put into English, or for that matter into any other language.

Why didn't *you* say yes?

I'll tell you why, Charentz.

Because you are more than an Armenian, more even than only another member of the human race. You are a poet, so shocked by the treachery of all men seeking to save their skins at any cost that only with the help of cocaine could you stay among them and pretend to be one of them.

God love them, as every poet is obliged to say, not with contempt but with charity. They all did, they are all doing, only what you advised me to do, which I have never done, which you never did.

*Adolf Hitler:* THERE ARE BADGE-MAKERS WHO HAVE
**a** large badge they sell for one dollar that says,
Adolf Hitler Is Alive in Germany. Most of their
other badges are funny or dirty, so it's not easy to
understand the message of this particular badge. Is
it meant to be funny, dirty, stupid, or something
else? Or is it meant to be political? Does the badge-
maker or the company that gave him the order to
manufacture the badge mean that Adolf Hitler is
actually alive in Germany, that he isn't dead, that
he didn't commit suicide, that he wasn't killed, and
that he is working underground to make a come-
back? Or does it mean a great many Germans in
Germany are alive who are so like Hitler they

might as well *be* Hitler? Or is it an even more subtle joke that is meant to remind people of what happens to big loudmouths who are positive they are right?

Never mind how the whole German nation could believe in you and your ideas, how could *you* believe in yourself and in your ideas? And at the same time carry on as if you were the original of Charlie Chaplin's pompous little loner, and as if you never knew there had ever been any such person as Charlie Chaplin? Is it possible that comedians are the biggest killers? The more you succeeded the funnier you became—Sudetenland, Austria, Czechoslovakia, Poland, Paris—you were hilarious, as each of them fell, but you couldn't cope with failure, the supreme province of all comedians. Failure only made you ugly, stupid, cowardly, ratty, and obscene.

*Are* you alive in Germany? You aren't alive in England. If you're alive in America, God help the Chinese.

*Carl Sandburg:* I REMEMBER OUR FIRST MEETING, in San Francisco, at the bookstore owned and operated by Leon Gelber and Theodore Lilienthal, on Sutter Street, in 1937, exactly thirty years ago, when you were fifty-nine, which is my present age, and I was twenty-nine.

Gelber, Lilienthal's was one of several bookstores I liked to go to in San Francisco in those days. Jack Newbegin's on Post Street was another. Paul Elder's was a third. As a new writer I liked to step into the stores and find out how my books were doing, and look at the new books that had come out, and chat with the owners and the clerks, and sometimes even meet a writer, although this was never something either to impel me to go to a bookstore or to keep me away.

One day, for instance, when I walked into Newbegin's, big cheerful loud-speaking Jack said, "You just missed Richard Halliburton."

I didn't know how to tell him it was all right.

Leon Gelber was one of my favorite people in San Francisco: keyed-up, enthusiastic, courteous, generous-hearted, and a good listener. There was more to him than met the eye, for he was one day found hanging by his neck, and everybody who had met him was surprised.

It was Leon who told me one summer afternoon when I walked into the store on Sutter Street, "Carl Sandburg's in the back room, do you want to meet him?"

And so we met. I suggested we go to a bar on Turk Street for a drink, because John Garfield was going to join me there. With John was somebody else, also a writer, and quite famous at the time, at least in Hollywood, but for the life of me I can't remember his name.

After two drinks at Joe Bailey's, where I used to play stud, you asked about the Cliff House, so we left the saloon and got into a taxi and drove out Geary to the Cliff House for a couple more drinks, all the while watching the seals on Seal Rock, and the ebb and flow of the ocean around the Rock.

Then, we took a taxi back to town, to Joe Vanessi's on Broadway near Pacific for some good Italian food. You were older than the rest of us, but you did just fine—talking, drinking, eating, and looking exactly the way you do in your photographs, exactly the way a poet ought to look—that is, simultaneously special, different, unique, but at the same time also casual, commonplace, and one of the people. The straw-colored hair of your head always stayed just a little awry, uncombed, apparently ignored.

Around eleven, after the Italian food and wine, we broke up, having all of us had a rather nice time. That is to say, you went home somewhere, to a hotel or to somebody's house where you were staying, and the writer whose name I can't remember said he had a big day tomorrow, and he began to walk home, and Garfield and I went up to Izzy's on Pacific Street.

"Imagine it," Garfield said, "a great man like that, a famous poet, an old guy, loafing around with a couple of kids from the slums, talking with us, drinking with us, eating with us, as if he were a kid from the slums, too. When I get to be his age I only hope I can be that young."

I was impressed, too. When I had been a telegraph messenger in Fresno, aged thirteen, working the nightshift after school, from four to midnight, I used to write poems on the company typewriters, because I had read everything on the poetry shelf at the public library—Walt Whitman, Vachel Lindsay, Edgar Lee Masters, and Carl Sandburg, among others, and I believed I ought to write stuff like that, too, but in the end it turned out that my first book was a collection of short stories, and after that I wrote fewer and fewer poems and hardly ever offered them to an editor, because for one thing there weren't many magazines to send poems to, and for another even if a magazine liked a poem they could pay only very little or nothing, and the very first thing I had to do was find out how to make a living at writing, so I wouldn't have to do other work.

Well, John Garfield died at the age of forty or so, at the height of a sensationally successful career as a movie star, and the writer whose name I can't remember, who was also a little under thirty when we all met, has faded away, which is either the same as dying or worse. And a lot of new poets and actors and story-writers have come along and taken their places among their kind, the new poets moving in the direction of Ezra Pound, T. S. Eliot, William Carlos Williams, and Wallace Stevens; the new actors taking their places beside Clark Gable, Humphrey Bogart, James Cagney, Paul Muni, Spencer Tracy, and Cary Grant; and the new story-writers moving in the direction of Ernest Hemingway, Scott Fitzgerald, William Faulkner, Morley Callaghan, and Stephen Vincent Benét.

That *was* America, in short. That was inno-
cent America, or ignorant America, or confused
America. And always, no matter how the history of
the nation changed, or what happened in Europe
and Asia, or who arrived or who departed, there
was news in the press about Carl Sandburg, and a
photograph, so that I was reminded of our happy
hours one summer day and night in San Francisco
long ago.

You played the guitar, you sang "The Blue-
tail Fly," you made records, you went to New
York, you went to Hollywood, you gave interviews
to newspaper and magazine writers, and at the
same time you finished the biggest biography of
Abraham Lincoln ever written.

In fact, I visited you overnight once at your
home in Harbert, Michigan, on the lake, not far
from Chicago, when you had just finished that
enormous work. We went for a walk in the evening to the house of a neighbor where a party was
going on—about thirty people of all ages, everybody having a good time, drinking, talking, laughing, listening to loud music on records, and there
you were, very tired after perhaps ten years of hard
work on the biography of one of the most com-
plicated Americans of all time. And you were
still just another plain ordinary man, with
two mops of unruly hair hanging over your fore-
head.

A young high-school girl brought her copy

of *The People, Yes,* and asked if you would autograph it for her. And you did, working at it, so that it would mean as much as possible to her.

And then you opened the book to the first page and began to read out loud.

The girl listened, I listened, somebody turned off the phonograph, everybody looked at you, everybody listened, everybody was delighted, everybody thought it was very kind of you not only to go to the party but to read one of your poems. They were dying to give you an ovation, their hands all ready to make loud applause the minute you stopped reading.

Now, here, they thought, was a good place to stop after five minutes of reading, but you didn't stop, you started reading another page.

You read well, in a deep earnest voice, saying the simple words as an actor would say them. The people at the party continued to be deeply impressed and grateful, and more than ever ready to give you the ovation you deserved for writing such powerful things about the people—the common people, the poor people, not people like themselves, upper middle class and even well-to-do.

One or two boys and girls, under fifteen, tiptoed away, but kids are kids and life comes before art with them, as of course it should.

Then, one or two of the younger adult couples quietly moved out of that great room, and very likely out of the house itself to where their own talk and laughter would not be a disturbance.

Then, two or three of the middle-aged couples found a way of leaving the room unobtrusively, until at last it was yourself, the girl you had signed the book for, and myself.

When you finished reading the whole book, it was only myself.

The People, Yes—but not the people at that party. You put the book down and we walked back to your house.

You met several Presidents, and you told me that somebody had approached you about accepting the nomination for the office of President—don't pass it along. Well, you certainly knew more about Lincoln than any other potential Presidential candidate. You met Marilyn Monroe and she loved you like a father. You were a consultant during the filming of the life of Jesus.

Yesterday when I read that you had died at your home in Flat Rock, North Carolina, I felt great sorrow, even though you had lived almost nine full decades, had had no failure or frustration, had never been accused of treason, never committed to a hospital for the insane, never been hated, despised, held in contempt, abandoned, hounded, misunderstood, misinterpreted, scorned, belittled, dishonored.

I felt sorry because somewhere along the

line the easy careless fall of the hair on your head, in two mops, right and left, had come to mean to the *people,* to use your term, poetry itself, American poetry, so that you yourself and your poetry and your other writing were taken to be great by the people who do not read poetry, prose, or anything else.

You lived and died famous, but actually unrecognized and unknown. The President himself issued a formal tribute to you which was written by somebody who had made a careful study of your verse. It sounded awfully important but didn't mean anything. You were probably a great man of some sort, but *that* couldn't have been the sort. Not that poets die young, although they do, no matter how long they live. They die real, and contrary to the misconception involved, not once, at the end, but many times right up to the end.

*Emory L. Ralston:* WHEN YOU FIRST TOLD ME THAT
you had changed your name to Emory L. Ralston,
I was puzzled, because your own name, Yedvard
Amircanian, or Edward Amircanian, or Eddie
American, as so many of your friends called you,
was such a good name. And why Emory? And what
was the L. for? And why Ralston?

  Last year about this time I made a special
trip to the Mall in Fresno, to where some new
fountain sculpture had just been put up, which
most people disliked because they said each of the
three pieces looked like some kind of accident
involving automobiles. I studied each of the three
metal and melted glass works, each well wrought,

each effective of its kind, and I began to walk north on the Mall so that I might pass the place where the Postal Telegraph Office had been, at 1036 Fulton Street, that is, where you and I had worked as messengers forty-five years ago.

And on my way there we came face to face, and you said, "Willie," and I said, "Eddie." We stopped to talk, our first talk in about thirty years, maybe even more. When some people I knew joined us, I introduced you as Emory L. Ralston, because the last time we met, at the Fair Grounds in Fresno, you said, "I'm not Yedvard Amircanian anymore, I'm Emory L. Ralston," and you gave me your card, which I kept and studied from time to time, although I remembered the new name instantly, perhaps that's why you chose it—it was unforgettable.

More unforgettable than your name, though, is your life, which is not known except in little bits and pieces by anyone excepting yourself. Your people, like my own, left Bitlis soon after the turn of the century and came to America. Your family and my family had known one another in Bitlis. You had the narrow intense face of the boys of Bitlis, and their eagerness to make good in the world. When you started work at the telegraph office you were a total stranger to me, but in less than half a day I knew you wanted desperately to keep your job, I knew that you were three years

older than me and that money had as much meaning in the life of your family as it did in the life of
mine. Both families needed money badly. You let it
be known at the outset that you intended to work
harder than any other messenger at that office, and
J. D. Tomlinson, the manager, was impressed. I had
always been the fastest messenger at that office, but
now I didn't mind at all if you took the honors. I
was still fast, but, as a number of relatives had suggested, I had decided it wasn't really necessary to
kill myself. Even J. D. one day said, "Ride your
bike a little more carefully. I've seen you out there
in the traffic. A few extra minutes won't hurt any
of us." The fact is the office needed at least two
more messengers, but there wasn't enough expense
money allotted to the office to permit J. D. to hire
two more. You got your job when Jake Somers
quit because the work was too hard.

    During our little talk on the Mall in Fresno
last year we asked and answered the usual questions. I was about to insist that we go to a bar for a
beer when the people came up, and while we were
all talking, you suddenly said, "I've got to go," and
you went. I was sure I'd find you nearby a little later,
but after the people went their way and I went on
up to 1036 Fulton, which is now a shoe store, and
stood there, remembering the old days at the
office, and then went back to find you, you were
gone.

At the Fair Grounds thirty years ago when you gave me your new name and your card, we had talked for only a few minutes, but I gathered that you had come to a kind of bad time in your life, and so I said, "Are you all right?" And then you told me a story about marrying a very pretty girl who was actually another man's girl. Between them, you said, they took you for everything—your savings, your house, your car. But she still phoned you now and then to ask for money to help her through some kind of new crisis. And you still met her and slept with her and gave her money. And you believed you must be crazy, or something.

And so when we met again, on the Mall, I wanted to hear about that. How had that situation resolved itself? During your marriage you had had no kids, so there was really no further claim the woman could make on you, and yet she continued to mean something very special to you. It was certainly special enough to give you ulcers. I went to the hospital where you died four months after our meeting on the Mall. I met an intern who knew the case, and he said it was ulcers. You arrived at the hospital in the middle of the night, and in less than six hours you were dead. It was something like the way it had been with an American writer I had heard about whose ulcers began to bleed in Madrid. Instead of going to bed and taking it easy, he packed a suitcase, took a taxi to the airport, waited for the plane, got on, flew to London, went to a hospital at one in the morning, and by daybreak was dead.

Yedvard Amircanian, Eddie American, Emory L. Ralston, I wish we had gone to a bar and talked, because I think I could have said something that might have been useful to you. Don't I have ulcers, too?

*Dr. Harold Fraser:* IN TIFLIS IN JUNE OF 1935 AT the Intourist Hotel I had a supper of miscellaneous native food, and three hours later I was deathly sick, but not too sick to go to the restaurant and tell the waiter in a loud voice that his restaurant was serving dirty food. If they expected to have tourists stopping in their city and eating at their restaurant, why didn't they learn to cook food that wouldn't make the tourists deathly sick? He didn't know, of course. He didn't know anything. What was all the shouting about in English? I bought a couple of bottles of water, believing they would be clean, took them to my room, and began to drink the water, because I didn't know how else to hope to get rid of the sickness. I had a very bad night, but I fetched three more bottles of water from the restaurant before going to bed and during the night I drank the water in all three bottles. In the morning I was pale, weak, wobbly, and irritable, but by evening matters were at least a little improved, and the next day I took a train and went to Erivan.

Three months later, back in San Francisco, the stomach was still giving me a bad time, but I kept drinking water and writing and trying to forget the stomach. I had rented a small room in an office building near Kearney Street, to see if I could write in an office, and one Saturday morning, running a slight fever, I wrote something called "The Man with the Heart in the Highlands." Sunday I was still running a fever, and Sunday night around two or three I knew something was seriously the matter. I remembered that my father had died of a ruptured appendix, so I got up, shaved, bathed, got dressed, and took a taxi to St. Francis Hospital.

A few tests were run, and then you came along, we had a short talk, and you said it was a definite attack of appendicitis, and so you'd attend to the matter immediately, which you did. At about eleven in the morning, an hour or two after the swollen appendix had been removed, I came to, feeling as if I had just been born into a grown man's body, aged twenty-seven, and I felt the most profound respect for the mere fact of being alive that I have ever felt, vowing to cherish every instant of my time and to keep myself in good health, pushing aside all of the stuff that only gives the body a bad time—cigarettes, whiskey, anxiety, impatience, excessive work, and so on.

But it didn't work out that way. And I am still so caught up in the limitations of my character that I smoke and drink and eat the wrong kind of food and never do any exercise except a little walking, and so my health is all shot—I'm fat, I've got ulcers, I'm impatient, I never sleep more than two hours at a time, wake up, read, sleep another hour or two, and so it goes all night every night except when I am so drunk I am anesthetized into four or five hours of sleep. That is how it is with me at the age of fifty-nine. I'm dying, most likely, but no more than I always have been, but what killed *you* at the age of forty-four, that's what I'd like to know.

*Benito Mussolini:* IN THE 1930s THERE WAS SCARCELY a newspaperman who hadn't been received by you in your great office, only slightly smaller than the office of Louis B. Mayer, at Metro-Goldwyn Mayer in Culver City. Everybody everywhere seemed to know your name and face and voice, from having seen you in action in newsreels, shouting from balconies to great gatherings of people in Rome. It was said that miscellaneous women, writers of poems and travel books, had also been received by you, knowing you drew no line and let them have all you had, by the clock, and fast. Not to mention a movie star or two, Italian or American. You were a cocky little fat boy with a thick neck and head, which in profile must have encouraged you to feel chosen: the man to restore the glory of Rome. And you did. *That* was its glory. The rest is writing.

The marvel is that you believed. You really believed the things that even historians began to suspect you might be bringing to pass. They could certainly see the fine highways you had working men build—proud men of the coming new Roman Empire. They could see the help you were sending to the poor. It wasn't much, it was temporary at best, but at least the poor were not quite so hopelessly poor, and they began to believe something might be happening, after all.

A man like George Bernard Shaw liked to say humorous but nice things about you. You couldn't be taken too seriously by a man like him, but at the same time you couldn't be hated. Everybody said something about you, mainly nice, or halfway nice, until the Spanish War, and then it began. You were no longer singing in a comic opera. You weren't a ten-cent tenor screaming from the bottom of your balls in a harmless little opera, you were a murderer. And then you decided to take on the Lion of Judah, and you weren't Mario Lanza, the American Screamer, you were Mr. Five Foot Two with Hands of Blood, and it was no fun trying not to hate you anymore. Even when Hitler treated you like a horse's ass, nobody felt sympathy for you.

When the clever boys abandoned you, and the working men of Italy caught up with you, you were *still* lugging your baggage around as if baggage is all, and it was pathetic. Hitler killed himself, at least. What happened to you had no dignity at all. You were the ten-cent tenor, after all.

*The Lion of Judah:* IN THOSE DAYS IT WAS TO THE
League of Nations that a small nation went with
its complaints, but of course the League had long
since fallen into uselessness, and you had no country, you had been driven out of your little country
by the Roman Comic Opera Singer, and nobody
had gone to your assistance, either to force him to
hold his horses, or to shoot them down as they
arrived, nobody wanted to help you, the world was
on its way to total disgrace and the problems of
the Lion of Judah and his country could not be
noticed with anything like outrage and concern.
You were photographed for the newsreels, and so
we saw you at the podium, and we heard what

you said to the nations of the world. It wasn't much. The most impressive thing about the war you lost was the story that you would use lions and tigers against the enemy—this appealed to children, but of course lions and tigers could do nothing in a war, if in fact they could do anything of that kind under *any* circumstances. Unless cornered, their instinct takes them straight away from human beings.

At last, however, your enemy was destroyed, the working people of his country were liberated, and your country was restored to itself, and to you. And you didn't look a lick different than you had ever looked. Mussolini was dead and disgraced, but you still had dignity and solemnity. And you were back in your old job.

You never told us very much about the job, though. You lived like a king, but rumors began to reach us that a lot of your people not only didn't live like kings, they didn't live like human beings— they had no regular source of food, no shelter, no clothing, no money, no jobs, no hospitals, no medical supplies, no schools, and in fact they had nothing except their country (also your country) under their feet, and the air and sky of their country around and above them. And the lions and tigers, which now and then in ignorance ate one or another of them, not knowing they were not Italian soldiers. And rumor began to come to us that you yourself not only had all of your dignity and solemnity, as if you might be a character of the Old Testament, but that you were also a very clever and very tough politician who put down enemies and rivals, including brothers and sons, with instant and awful finality. No head was chopped off, but it might as well have been.

Well, what it seems to come to is that to keep a country, to maintain a nation and a people, even without ever really improving anything for anybody, is a very hard job. It takes a lot of attention to detail, but we do know that you made it, you are in fact the Lion of Judah, the King of Abyssinia, although we are no longer impelled to take off our hat to you.

*Jacob Ahbood:* IN THE ANCIENT-HISTORY CLASS AT
Longfellow Junior High School in Fresno forty-
five years ago you sat across the aisle from me, a
dark son of Assyrian immigrants who had come to
California from Worcester, and you hated ancient
history so much you kept cracking your knuckles.

Every now and then I had to say, "Cut it
out, will you?"

This always surprised you, and you said,
"I'm sorry."

But three or four minutes later, crack-crack-
crack-crack again.

I don't know why you didn't like ancient
history. It was just as easy as any of the other

classes. It was about kings and slaves a long time ago, in the olden places of the world. One king would lay low and catch another king by surprise and beat the shit out of him, but you never seemed to get the hang of the thing, and you always seemed afraid that Miss Harrigan was going to ask you a question and you wouldn't know the answer.

Did I say Miss Harrigan? Hell, that wasn't her name. It was something else. A little woman, not old, nervous as a ferret, and subject to fits of exhausted anger, suddenly throwing up her hands and screaming that she simply would not, *could* not go on if nobody was going to respond to her teaching.

But of course I was under orders *never* to respond, from having always responded instantly, but with the kind of answers and remarks that only made trouble for her. She expected somebody like *you* to help her, but you never did. You just sat there brooding and cracking your knuckles, which was really her big problem in that class, although she never found out.

From where she stood the cracking was not so loud or annoying as from where I sat, but it reached her, too, and in the end she found herself totally unable to go on—and blamed me, as silent as I had been, watching her make a fool of herself, and listening to you cracking your knuckles.

She was always sure I had put a jinx on her somehow, and so she would look at me with more hatred in her eyes than any of the old Babylonians, Sumerians, Akkadians, Hittites, or Assyrians had ever had for one another, and I would look down at my open book, like a polite American.

You should have stopped cracking your knuckles and you should have tried to help that teacher by taking an interest in the fascinating things she was telling us about all of those crazy people in our part of the world.

One of the things you might have noticed was that the drawing in the book of one of the Assyrians who beat up the Babylonians resembled you perfectly, because that would have given you confidence, and she would have felt that her teaching was getting through to somebody. But no, you wanted to be an American, like me, like Joe Sargon, like Avak Amadouni, like Haig Mamigonian—hell, we'd been in Fresno from the beginning, while you'd been in Worcester, you couldn't be an American like us, you should have been satisfied to be an Assyrian like the guy in the book.

I'll tell you one thing, you didn't just drive her crazy, you drove me crazy, too, with your fantastic nervousness, embarrassment, and your ferocious determination to be an American. I was glad when I graduated from that stupid class, because I didn't have to have you next to me cracking your knuckles all the time. So you made it at last—you became an American, a used-car salesman, and then you got the whole Ford agency for Visalia—good for you, Jacob Ahbood, but forget it.

*Dr. Anoushavan Chomp:* I WAS SELLING PAPERS on the corner of the Republican Building one Friday evening in 1919 when you came to me and spoke in Armenian, saying, "Come to 222 O Street tomorrow morning at ten o'clock and you will have the honor of being the first boy to sell a new paper in Fresno."

You spoke high-flown Armenian, you yourself were high-flown, but I understood your words and to some extent you yourself. You were from somewhere else, and later I heard you had gotten out literary weeklies in Sofia, Bucharest, Cairo, and Paris. I knew you were an intellectual from the fact that you called one or two local men who were escorting you around town *ideyote,* which I thought was your way of pronouncing an English word, but learned later was an Armenian word, and in fact there were those who said *ideyote* originated in the Armenian language and became "idiot" in the English. You wore a black cape with a red lining, and a black hat with a very wide brim, a red scarf, gray spats, and you carried a walking stick. What you had was a haughty style of behavior and speech, and what you didn't have was money.

Saturday was always the worst day of the week for me, so I decided to take you up, and when I reached the plain little house at 222 O Street at ten the next morning, there you were, busy with bundles of the paper you wanted me to have the honor of being the first to sell in the streets of Fresno. It was a good-looking piece of printing, on white paper, with the name of it in ornate Armenian type across the top of the front page: *Tsahkh-ahvel,* a word I hadn't heard, which I was later told meant, literally, Wrong Broom, or Left-handed Broom, but actually meant several other things, along the lines of misunderstanding, or being busy in a useless way, or working hard for nothing, and so on.

"Well," you said. "Take fifty copies and go straight to the coffeehouses—the Ararat and the Arax, and then go to the places where you know Armenians go on Saturday—the Free Market, the grocery stores, and the street corners. Sell them all and come back for more. The paper is worth a quarter, but the price is only five cents. Every Armenian in town will buy a copy."

I knew you were dreaming, but I didn't say anything. I asked a few basic questions—what is it about? How often does it come out?

"Armenian life in dispersion is what it's about," you said, "and it comes out every Saturday morning."

As I was going down the steps of the house two other Armenian boys who sold *The Evening Herald* were coming up the street, so I knew you had asked every Armenian newsboy in town to sell your paper, *Tsahkh-ahvel.*

I ran to the Ararat, which was jam-packed with men playing cards and backgammon and drinking small cups of coffee. Everybody took an interest in the new paper, quite a few borrowed copies, turned pages, read something, laughed, and handed the paper back. Nobody paid a nickel for a copy, to have, to take home, to read, to keep, or to throw away. Frankly, this surprised me, because while I didn't expect farmers to throw away a nickel on some kind of humorous paper, I knew a lot of intellectuals went to the Ararat and I was sure at least one or two would want to buy a copy, to examine at their leisure, so they could talk about it.

The situation was the same at the Arax, and

worse at the Free Market, where most of the fruit
and vegetable stands were owned and operated by
Armenians. The other people wondered what all
the shouting was about, for I tried to sell the paper
as if it were no different than an American newspaper, hollering, *"Tsahkh-ahvel, Tsahkh-ahvel,"*
which the Armenians knew meant wrong broom,
left-handed broom, or you've got it all misunderstood.

Dr. Chomp, I tried very hard to sell fifty
copies of *Tsahkh-ahvel,* even to Americans, but I
failed. At one o'clock I knew it was useless to try
anymore. I had run into five other Armenian boys
racing around town shouting *"Tsahkh-ahvel,"* but
not one of them had sold a copy, either, excepting
Sunnar Giragosian, whose uncle had bought a copy
to encourage him. When I reached the house at 222
O Street you were gone. An old woman of the
neighborhood who was doing your housekeeping
said you would be back in the evening. "How
many did you sell?"

"Not one."

She told me to set the papers down on the
table in the parlor. I asked if I could take one
home, and she said, "The price is five cents each,
of course." I told her I didn't have a nickel, so
then she said, "Very well, take one on credit—you
can pay the great doctor another time."

"Who is he?" I said.

"Who *is* he?" she said with astonishment and annoyance. "He is Dr. Anoushavan Chomp, not a simple doctor who gives people useless pills, he is a doctor of philosophy, graduated from a high university."

I took the paper home, and that evening my mother examined it when she came home from packing figs at Guggenheim's.

"It's very funny," she said. "And you weren't able to sell one copy? Well, next Saturday try again, and be sure to bring a copy home."

But that was it, there was only the one issue. *Tsahkh-ahvel* folded, and you disappeared. I have always wondered about that whole business.

*L. B. Mayer:* WHAT WAS THE B. FOR? THE L. WAS for Louis, I believe, but I never did find out what the B. was for, although a writer I was once drinking with who had had a very bad time trying to do a shooting script for you, made a few guesses about what the B. was for, but he was drunk and poor, having lost his job and being driven to spending the principal, against the advice of his mother, his lawyer, his tax expert, his accountant, his business manager, and his agent, all of whom told him, "Be careful, hard times will come, $600,000 can't last forever, you know."

Any time I had $600 I lived like a millionaire and hated nobody, but then writers vary, as they say. One man needs a million dollars to feel safe, another needs no more than walking-around money. You needed six or seven million dollars, and a lot of other things, but how safe did you ever really feel, considering where you were and who you had to work with. If you felt totally safe, it must have come as an awful surprise suddenly that you were dead, because it was an awful surprise to me when I read that you were dead, and I wasn't even remotely somebody who might have contributed to the likelihood of that event. I was only one of six or seven hundred writers who had at one time or another visited you in your office and had made a deal and gone to work on some fantasy or other you were sure would be just the fantasy the doctor ordered—for moneymaking. Your comrades Eddie Mannix, Sam Katz, Benny Thau, and the three or four others whose names I can't remember, they all went to your expensive funeral, but what's going to a funeral compared to being the star of one? Nothing, a little nuisance, at best, and then back to the old fight.

To tell you the truth, I really don't see how it could have happened. It doesn't ring true. It wasn't you. It was somebody else. Why should you die? You ate the best food, drank the best water and wine, wore the best clothes, knew the most important people in the whole country—even the President himself sometimes phoned you to

ask a small favor, like, "Make a picture to encourage American boys to be movie-star heroes in
the Army, Navy, Marine Corps, Coast Guard, and
National Guard." And you did, you always did little favors like that for anybody important who
phoned and asked you to. The writer who claimed
to know what the B. was for, who had a dozen different variations of the sort of thing it was probably
for, worked for six long months on just a story like
that—but you didn't like it, because how could your
biggest moneymaking star, Mr. Clark Gable, play
the part of a Mexican boy who volunteered the day
after Pearl Harbor and had so much trouble in the
Army about being Mexican that he finally went
over the hill and took to living a life of crime? Or
at any rate that was all I seem to remember about
the story the writer worked on for six months,
although he told it to me steadily for a full hour.
The minute I read in the paper that you had died
I thought, "Don't believe it, it's a trick, there's a
tax-avoidance angle in it somewhere, he's gone to
Havana to make some more money in a new and
easier arena."

For you to be dead didn't make sense. The
fact is it was un-American, and if you stood
for anything it was for the simple dignity of
not being un-American—ever. Let Eddie Mannix
die and have a big funeral, let Sam Katz die,
let Benny Thau die, but don't expect L. B.

Mayer to do a silly thing like that, at the last minute.

Those fellows were good competent assistants, but you were the fellow they assisted, you were the one who allowed them the honor of assisting you, you couldn't do all your brilliant business alone, somebody had to give you a little assistance, so you let those fellows do it, and paid them big money, too.

They certainly assisted you in the deal you made with me, and if you want to know the truth, ten years after your disappearance—you're not dead, I know you're not, you can't be, or else why would they be still so devoted to your principles of procedure?—ten years after your disappearance they're still assisting you.

When I got out of the Army and offered to pay back to you, to Metro-Goldwyn-Mayer, the $60,000 you paid me for *The Human Comedy*, what do you think your assistants said?

Your old protégé Benny Thau said, "We don't want to sell."

I said, "Keep the millions of dollars in profit you made from the phony movie you made from my story. Keep the print. Just let me pay back every cent you paid me, so I can own my own writing again and do what I please with it."

"No, sir," your assistants said, "drop dead, foolish writer."

Writers are fools to your assistants, you know, because a few measly dollars can buy them, as you know, having bought so many of them, but the whole point is you didn't buy me, and you didn't even buy my story, you told me you wanted to make a movie of *The Human Comedy* because it was such a good and true American story, but you said it would lose money. You wanted to do a patriotic thing, and you didn't want me to prevent you from doing such a thing. You made money by the millions from other nonpatriotic stories, but this was going to be something you wanted to do for the nation, something you had to do for America. Well, you did it all right, but it wasn't patriotic, and it wasn't for America, it was for China, I believe, and it didn't lose money, it made millions of dollars, and it's still making money for you, so why should I believe you died?

You got a nice big chunk of money from the busy boy of television who made a television show out of it, too, and over the years he's made a lot of money, and feels safe, too. Just last year he told somebody writing for a magazine that while he is really interested in the nation and politics, the reason he isn't going into politics is that with only a little better than two million dollars to his name, how long would that last in politics?

You are sitting on my writing, and you won't let it be patriotic for me, too, won't let me be a patriot and make a film of the story the way it should have been made in the first place, so I can have a million or two of the same kind of patriotic dollars you go right on sitting on.

L. B., don't ever believe them, that wasn't you at your funeral, that wasn't you they buried, that was a ringer, you're still out there rounding up the patriotic money, as hale and hearty as ever.

*Anybody:* WE MET IN OSLO IN 1935, AGAIN IN ANY number of other cities, from early in September of 1908, in Fresno, to yesterday, July 31, 1967, in Paris. You were never a stranger, although I had no idea who you were.

So don't go, but if you must, say hello to everybody.